BEWIGGED AND BEWILDERED?

Misunderstandings and jargon prevent many from seriously considering a career as a barrister in the belief that such a career is not for them or that they are not for it. Others know that they might want to become barristers but not how to go about it, or just want to know more about this somewhat mysterious profession. This book (by a barrister who was formerly a university law lecturer) clearly but informally explains the traditions, terminology and institutions of the Bar, and what it is actually like to be a barrister. With this aim, several barristers practising in different fields describe in detail a typical week in their life. Advice is then given on how to be accepted into, fund and survive the various academic and other stages that precede qualification as a barrister, including work experience, Bar School, and pupillage (the barrister's apprenticeship). Space is also given to how to transfer to the Bar after another legal or non-legal career.

PORTLAND, OREGON

Published in North America (US and Canada) by
Hart Publishing
c/o International Specialized Book Services
920 NE 58th Avenue, Suite 300
Portland, OR 97213-3786
USA
Tel: +1 503 287 3093 or toll-free: (1) 800 944 6190
Fax: +1 503 280 8832
E-mail: orders@isbs.com
Website: www.isbs.com

Hart Publishing, 16C Worcester Place, OX1 2JW
Telephone: +44 (0)1865 517530 Fax: +44 (0)1865 510710
E-mail: mail@hartpub.co.uk
Website: http://www.hartpub.co.uk

British Library Cataloguing in Publication Data
Data Available

ISBN-13: 978-1-84113-651-6 (paperback)

Typeset by Hope Services, Abingdon
Printed and bound in Great Britain by
TJ International Ltd, Padstow, Cornwall

Dedicated to my wife.

FOREWORD

The English Bar plays a vital role in our society. So long as our democracy survives, and so long as disputes between citizens, or between the citizen and the state, continue to be resolved after each side has had its say, so long will there be a need for presentational skills, for drafting skills, and for objective advice: in other words for the forms of expertise which the Bar, both employed and self employed, routinely displays.

However, as Chairman of the Bar for the past year (and barrister, silk, head of chambers, and leader of a circuit before that) I have come to realise that of all the challenges and upheavals that the Bar faces—and there are many—none is so important as the need to ensure that the Bar attracts the brightest women and men of integrity and ability, whatever their social and ethnic origins. It is time that more people were let in on the secrets of practice at the Bar. Accordingly, I endorse Adam Kramer's unique book for throwing open the doors of the Bar to current and future generations, and I hope that, by giving the confidence that can come only from being fully informed, it will bring readers to this most enjoyable, worthwhile, and rewarding of vocations. I only wish it had been available to me when I started in practice 35 years ago.

Stephen Hockman QC
London
December 2006

CONTENTS

Introduction to This Book

Everyone knows a little about barristers, whose ancient profession is well respected in society and well represented in literature. Yet few people who don't have one in their family know much about what barristers really do and where they do it, except perhaps that they wear wigs and argue in court like Rumpole or Kavanagh. That, however, will be enough for many to gain at least the suspicion that they might want to try their hand as a barrister themselves. But what then? When I thought I might like to become a barrister I was in a better position to find out about the job than most, because I went to the sort of school and the sort of university that produce a fair few of them. Even so, where I would have expected an abundance of information I found very little. Being the cautious type of person who goes to find a book on something before undertaking it, my next step was naturally to look for a suitable book that could help me. As far as I could see there was none (or at least none that had been written in the last 20 years). I then had to face the wall of terms and acronyms alone. For example I learned that I could have done a non-law degree followed by a CPE or GDL, or alternatively a senior status law degree or exempting law degree, but in any event that after my completing my BA or LLB in law I had to do a BVC, join an Inn, obtain a pupillage in a set of chambers through OLPAS (after doing mini-pupillages), get called to the Bar and get tenancy and so begin practice (and then my CPD points began). Not self-explanatory.

I nevertheless made it into practice as a barrister, and wrote this book to guide the way. My aim is a modest one. As one author has observed:

> Half the battle is to become familiar with your surroundings, the other half is to know the technical terms. Every profession has its jargon, and the law is no different.

> (Harold Morris, *The Barrister* (London, 1930) at p 36)

I hope that when you have read this book you will understand what it is actually like to be a barrister in England and Wales[1]—what a barrister does from day to day, in what surroundings, and for what reward. I want the reader to understand the process by which a person becomes a barrister, including, above all, that strange, strange year of the pupillage (the barrister's apprenticeship). When you have finished, you will understand all the jargon and arcane customs (and with that in mind, the glossary section at the back of the book may be the most useful part of this work—all the terms in bold in the main text are explained in that glossary), and you will know where to go for further information (these days, the answer is invariably the Web; see the sources listed in the 'Further Information' section near the back of the book).

It will then be for the reader, who knows his or her character and circumstances, to decide whether to seek to become a barrister. For myself, though, I can't think of a more enjoyable and rewarding profession. If you do decide to become a barrister then you can read about the stages you will face (see also the 'Timetables for Routes to the Bar' at the back of the book) and be forearmed, knowing how much money it will take, what you'll need to do in advance so that your CV and application are as required, and how to make the various other choices that need to be made.

THE COMPANION WEBSITE

For occasional updates please visit:
http://www.hartpub.co.uk/updates/bewigged-updates.html

CORRECTIONS AND IMPROVEMENTS

This book paints a wide range of institutions, practices and professions with a broad brush, and covers matters that are not easy to research, at

---

[1] The systems in Northern Ireland and Scotland are different and beyond the scope of this book: see http://www.barlibrary.com/ for Northern Ireland and http://www.advocates.org.uk/ for Scotland. Both also have split professions (as explained below in chapter one) with between 500–600 barristers in each jurisdiction (although they are called 'advocates' in Scotland).

least by conventional means. It has also been written at a time of numerous (as yet incomplete) changes to the Bar and its organisations. Inevitably, therefore, inaccuracies or unintentional misrepresentations will have crept into the book. My publisher and I welcome suggestions for corrections, improvements, and modifications that may assist in any future editions. Please email such comments to bewigged@ hartpub.co.uk or write to Hart Publishing, 16C Worcester Place, Oxford, OX1 2JW, UK.

THANKS

When I started planning this book during pupillage it was an exercise in therapy, but when I wrote it during my first year or so as a barrister and husband it was a distraction. I must therefore thank my chambers and my wife, Kathryn, for putting up with the distraction. I must also thank my friends for their anecdotes, which I have shamelessly mined over the last year or two. More than that, though, I must thank those who have contributed sections to the 'Week in the Life' chapter, and those who have read and commented upon drafts of the book and answered my queries: my wife (who had the small matter of her doctoral thesis to deal with but still found the time), Tim Akkouh, Tony Beswetherick, Justin Davis, Hugh Derbyshire, Rebecca Deutsch, Mark Dobbs, Timothy Dutton QC, Tessa Hetherington, Stephen Hockman QC, Andy Hood, Professor Adrian Keane, Dr Richard Langer, Charlie Lees, Sarah Lewis, Andrew Onslow QC, Bhavna Patel, Sarah McCann, Sarah Prager, the Honourable Mr Justice Stephen Silber, Christopher Symons QC and Mike Thomas. Finally, I must thank Richard my publisher. Is there another publisher that is so clearly on the side of the angels? I hope never to have to find out.

Adam Kramer, autumn 2006

1

Introduction to the English Bar

BARRISTERS AND SOLICITORS

Unlike in America, but not dissimilar to **practice** in Europe, the English legal profession is what is referred to as a 'split profession'. This means that there are two types of English lawyer: solicitors and barristers.[2] **Solicitors** are overwhelmingly the primary legal professionals in that there are more of them, cases come to them first, and they are the more important in the vast majority of cases. There are about 100,000 solicitors in England and Wales as compared with about 15,000 barristers. Of these barristers, 3,000 are at the Employed Bar (see later) and the rest are self-employed, which mode of operation was, until recently, referred to as being 'at the independent Bar'. We'll talk more about why being self-employed is important to what a barrister does and the working environment he or she does it in. While we're dealing with terminology, you should know that while lawyers in the US are called **attorneys**, that term has not been used in the UK since the nineteenth century. Two terms you do need to know are counsel, which is another word for barrister or barristers (counsel is both the singular and the plural), and the Bar, which is the collective term for all barristers.

---

[2] At the risk of confusing matters, I should point out there is a third branch of the legal profession, namely legal executives. Generally these work in solicitors' firms doing similar (although often more junior) work to solicitors. However, unlike solicitors, legal executives do not have to take a law degree and Legal Practice Course, and usually become trainee legal executives straight from completing a non-law degree and then qualify as legal executives over the next three or four years, while working.

> **Lawyers in England and Wales**
> 100,000 solicitors
>   (of whom 3,300 are **solicitor-advocates**)
> 15,000 barristers
>   (of whom 12,000 are self-employed and 3,000 are at the
>   Employed Bar)
>   (of whom 10,000 are in London and 5,000 are outside London)
> 22,000 **legal executives**

The key to understanding the interaction between barristers and solicitors is knowing that, normally speaking, clients (ordinary people who are not lawyers) cannot go directly to barristers for help but must go to solicitors. Solicitors can then get a barrister involved if appropriate. The Bar is a 'referral profession'; as one author puts it, solicitors are 'the GPs of the legal profession', leaving barristers as the specialists (Charlotte Buckhaven, *Barrister by and Large* (London, Pan Books, 1985), p 11). However, it should be remembered that this split professional aspect of the law is important only to **litigation** (meaning legal disputes, as opposed to other general situations in which people may want advice on how to act within the law): in most transactional work (buying a house, merging companies, drafting contracts, managing company employment policies, advising on tax) solicitors do everything and barristers have little or no involvement, at least until the legal dispute arises. Much lower court litigation and non-court litigation (such as **arbitration**) is also handled by solicitors. However, within the relevant fields of litigation in which barristers primarily operate, barristers can be said to be specialists in three broad areas:

The first thing barristers are specialists in is the law. This may seem strange as solicitors are also lawyers and have studied the law for the same number of years and at the same universities as barristers. However, solicitors, particularly young solicitors, spend a large amount of their time collecting evidence and generally administering and managing a transaction, inquiry, trial, or project. Barristers get to spend more time working on legal points, and their expertise builds up accordingly, and so solicitors often come to barristers for advice on points of law (although there are many solicitors whose knowledge of the law is at least the equal of that of most barristers and who handle most or all legal points themselves).

The second thing barristers are specialists in is court practice and procedure. Again, because solicitors are often tied up with collecting evidence and general management of the case, barristers are often more familiar with the tactics, procedures, and rules of evidence of litigation and trials and other court **hearings**. This means that they have a better feel for what would happen if a case were to go to court, and are better able to make strategic decisions concerning the litigation (what applications to make to the court, what witnesses to rely on, what questions to ask, how much to offer in settlement). As with any generalisation, this does not always apply: many solicitors' firms have specialist litigation departments and the solicitors in those departments may be as expert at litigation or law as barristers, or more so, and further, as is explained below, a large portion of lower court litigation is handled without the use of barristers. To make matters more confusing, some types of barrister do little or no litigation (such as tax barristers and a certain type of **Chancery** barrister: this terminology will be explained later).

The third thing barristers are specialists in is **advocacy**: arguing and presenting cases in court. Partly because of the other demands on solicitors' time that have already been mentioned, in general barristers are more expert in advocacy than solicitors and so are often **instructed** by solicitors to conduct in court the litigation that the solicitors' clients are involved in (in other words, making applications and speeches and asking questions of witnesses). Although many barristers spend more time out of court than in court, advocacy skills, taught at **Bar school** and by the **Inns of Court** and Specialist Bar Associations (see below), remain the distinguishing skills of the Bar.[3] All barristers, no matter how junior, automatically (ie from their first day in practice and without further examinations) have the right to speak in all courts of the land. Solicitors automatically have the right to speak in the lower courts (magistrates' courts and county courts) and, given the number

---

[3] It should perhaps be added that court hearings are more important in England and Wales than in many other jurisdictions. Although there are lots of documents required in litigation, the oral hearing plays a larger part in English and Welsh litigation than in litigation in some other jurisdictions. Further, the advocate's role in England and Wales is more important than in many other jurisdictions because, whereas in many countries in Europe the judge has a major role in the investigation of the case and the questioning of witnesses and determination of legal issues (the so-called 'inquisitorial system'), in England and Wales the lawyers are responsible for collecting all the evidence, and the advocates are responsible for asking questions of the witnesses in court and arguing about the correct legal principles (the so-called 'adversarial system'). As a result, advocacy and understanding the court process are of pre-eminent importance in England and Wales.

of solicitors, it is therefore not surprising that most advocacy in those courts is conducted by solicitors and not by barristers. Furthermore, for the last 10 years solicitors have been able to earn **higher rights of audience** (the rights to **appear** not only in the lower courts but also in the Crown Courts, High Court, Court of Appeal, and House of Lords) by passing further examinations and qualifying as what are known as **solicitor-advocates**. However, so far only about 3,300 solicitors have qualified as solicitor-advocates (see further below), and the upshot is that most hearings in the higher courts, as well as some in the lower courts, are conducted by barristers.

The solicitor—being the primary legal practitioner—is generally in charge of the case and of liaising with the client, and brings in barristers as sub-contractors for the specialist work described above (just as a builder might have a contract to construct a building and will sub-contract part of the work to an electrician or roof specialist). The consequence of this is that the barrister's clients are in fact solicitors, who are his or her paymasters (unless the government is paying under the legal aid schemes) and the ones to whom the barrister is providing the service, although the barrister also has duties to the client who is employing the solicitor, that is, the non-lawyer for whom all this is happening (who is distinguished from the solicitors by the label '**lay client**': 'lay' simply means non-professional).

Bizarrely, however, barristers have traditionally not entered into contracts with solicitors for their services and fees and have instead worked on an honour system (although on standard terms set by the **Bar Council** and **Law Society**), meaning that solicitors cannot be sued if they don't pay up, and that interest does not accrue even if solicitors are late paying their invoices. This contributes to cash-flow problems, discussed elsewhere, since, although solicitors almost always pay up, they often take a long time to do so. Since 1991 barristers have been allowed to enter into contracts with solicitors (rather than using this honour system), but this remains the exception, although negotiations between the Bar Council and Law Society to make a contract the default position are fairly advanced and are likely to lead to a change in the near future.

Although solicitors can usually do nicely without engaging a barrister, most cases cannot proceed without a solicitor. Indeed, the barristers' **Code of Conduct** (more about this later) forbids barristers from holding money on behalf of lay clients, conducting correspondence or interviewing witnesses, and settling witness statements. Only solicitors, or the lay client in person, may conduct these tasks (although, as with any rule, it is not as black and white as this suggests).

When a solicitor gives a barrister a case, the solicitor is said to give the barrister a **brief**, or to **instruct** the barrister: a brief takes the form of a set of instructions to the barrister to answer a particular question, draft a particular document, or to represent the lay client at a particular hearing. Traditionally, the brief is tied up with a ribbon (often pink).

SETS OF CHAMBERS

Solicitors work in law **firms**. These will be legal partnerships of one form or another, but basically firms are like companies, sometimes very big companies.

In contrast, the majority of barristers are self-employed (the minority who are not are discussed below) but usually gather together into an association (ie not a company) and rent offices from which they work, and share the costs of secretaries (although they have far fewer than solicitors), receptionists, stationery, marketing, **clerks** (see below), and perhaps a library and conference rooms.

The association (and the offices the barrister works in) is called a '**chambers**' (treated as a singular: 'where is your chambers?', 'I'm on my way back to chambers'), also known as a '**set**' or '**set of chambers**' (as in 'which set are you in?'). The name of a set will usually be its street address ('3 Verulam Buildings', '7 Bedford Row', '9 Old Square'), although nowadays more modern names are becoming common ('Matrix Chambers', 'Landmark Chambers').[4] In some chambers all barristers have their own room, whereas in others, particularly in areas of the law which involve a lot of court-work (and so less time spent in chambers), barristers share rooms with one or two other barristers. Generally each individual barrister rents a room (or a share in it) from chambers, which, in turn, rents or owns the chambers' building. In London the chambers usually rents its building from the **Inn** it is situated in.

Chambers generally have one or two **heads of chambers**, who will be selected from the most senior barristers in the chambers. A small

---

[4] By way of contrast, it should be noted that self-employed barristers in Northern Ireland and Scotland do not work in chambers but rather are one-man bands working out of what they call a 'library' system.

chambers would have 10 to 20 barristers in it, a large chambers 50 to 60, with the majority of sets falling somewhere in between. Even a large chambers, however, is dwarfed by a big law firm, which can be an international organisation with thousands of lawyers spread throughout the world. Because a barrister is associated with the other barristers in his chambers, all the members benefit if a set has a good reputation, which is one reason why barristers spend time and money on attracting good pupils. Many sets find it useful if all their barristers specialise in particular areas of work so that their reputation is also specialised, and solicitors may get into the habit of going to a particular set with a particular type of case, even if the individual barristers they know are unavailable or too senior. While many sets still do the full range of work, specialisation is increasing and, in particular, a large number of sets do either criminal law or civil law (which means everything except criminal law) but not both. I am in a commercial law chambers and will, therefore, never handle a criminal case.

The common chambers specialisms are the following:

(i)   Chancery law: specialising in property, trusts, taxation, and wills.
(ii)   common law: a mixture of civil law work and often crime, that is, pretty much everything, often with an emphasis on personal injury work.
(iii)   commercial law: specialising in the law of commerce, that is, business and trade (especially contracts, insurance, banking, shipping, etc) and company matters.
(iv)   commercial Chancery law: specialising in Chancery matters but with a commercial flavour (above all, company and insolvency law).
(v)   criminal law: specialising in crime.
(vi)   family law: specialising in family law.
(vii)   intellectual property law: the law of patents, copyrights, and trademarks.
(viii) public law: specialising in administrative law, human rights, and planning law.

A good idea of the types of things barristers specialise in can be gleaned from a list of the Specialist Bar Associations for the private Bar (clubs that hold conferences, lectures, and training events and represent the interests of their members): ALBA (the Constitutional and Administrative Law Bar Association); the Chancery Bar Association; COMBAR (the Commercial Bar Association); the

Criminal Bar Association; the Employment Law Bar Association; FLBA (the Family Law Bar Association); IPBA (the Intellectual Property Bar Association); the Parliamentary Bar Mess; PIBA (the Personal Injuries Bar Association); PEBA (the Planning and Environment Bar Association); the Professional Negligence Bar Association; the Property Bar Association; the Revenue Bar Association; and TECBAR (the Technology and Construction Bar Association). You certainly do not need to know these acronyms.

IT'S NOT JUST ABOUT LAW

Having explained chambers specialisms, this is a convenient point at which to explain something that is fundamental to the practice of the law, namely that law is only half of the picture. The law is a regulatory system that applies to all fields of human endeavour. Like many other service industries (accountancy, marketing, etc), but to a greater degree, the law gets deeply into all areas of society. As a result, there are two ways of looking at law and barristers, and accordingly two ways of coming at the question of whether you want to be a barrister. You may start at the law end, deciding that the law itself interests you, that you have the skills that a barrister needs, and that you are interested in doing the sorts of things that lawyers do (**advocacy** in court, drafting documents, solving difficult intellectual or practical problems).

Alternatively, however, you may come at law from the other end of the microscope. You may be somebody who is interested by a particular field of society, such as science, medicine, crime and investigation, commerce, the environment and planning, immigration and asylum, employment, family relationships, or tax and finances. However, you may not want to go into those fields by the ordinary route, (respectively) as a scientific researcher, doctor, police officer, business employee, lobbyist or charity or council worker, trade union or human resources worker, counsellor, or accountant. You may instead prefer to go in from a different angle, as a barrister, doing (respectively) intellectual property, medical negligence and personal injury law, criminal or prison law, commercial and **Chancery** law, environmental and planning law, immigration and human rights law, employment law, family law, or tax law. All barristers practise in one or more of these areas, or areas like them, which means that barristers become acquainted with the workings of these areas of society and are actually involved participants in those areas. A criminal and family lawyer spends a lot of time with probation officers and social workers and their reports; a tax barrister spends a lot of time with accounts; a patent lawyer spends a lot of time with patents and other scientific documents.

Becoming a barrister therefore enables you to practise in a field of society that interests you, while doing so in special circumstances that are different to those in which most people in that field (doctors, police officers, council workers, etc) work. On the whole, barristers are self-employed, have pretty good earnings, work in a particular environment and with particular hours (which are different from those of a police officer, doctor, etc), and face the further challenges that the law provides that other people in a field of society do not face (although some of those in the list above work with the law almost as much as barristers do). Being a barrister also enables you to broaden your field somewhat. Whereas a hospital doctor or council worker or accountant (or whatever) will inevitably end up working with a limited range of problems in a limited range of circumstances (gynaecology in a hospital, or planning in the west of Sheffield, or auditing manufacturing companies), barristers get to do a broader range of things. Even a barrister specialising in medical negligence will probably deal with the full range of medical services (GPs, hospital doctors, specialists, nurses, anaesthetists, paramedics) and also deal with cases of dentistry and veterinary negligence, will probably also do some other work (such as cases involving injuries following accidents in the workplace), and will often represent both patients and doctors. As a commercial barrister I have had to become intimately acquainted with areas as varied as siphonic drainage of roofs, film finance, automated computerised inter-bank payments, securitisation, high-performance cars, life insurance selling, and payroll computer software. I do not mean only that I have had to know about the law of these areas, although of course that is true; I mean I have had to know about these areas themselves, since a barrister cannot set out or defend a claim for negligence or ask the right questions of a witness (for example) without knowing the background and circumstances of the case and its setting very well.

Many people come to the Bar through an interest in the law and find themselves gravitating towards a chambers that operates in a field that interest them, and then, within that chambers, focusing their practice into an even narrower field that over time they find they prefer. Personally, I developed an interest in the law and particularly the law of contracts during my law degree, had always fancied being involved in commerce but didn't fancy working for a big company or starting a company of my own, and so ended up in commercial law. Probably I will end up specialising further, into insurance, banking, professional negligence, or some other area. Others, particularly those with non-law degrees, often skip the first step of choosing the law and jump straight to the step of choosing an area of legal practice. Therefore it is important to bear in mind that the relevant field in which a barrister works is not just important because of the ways in which it affects the barrister's working conditions (pay, hours, how much the barrister is in court and how much work is done on paper). It is also important because the relevant field in which a barrister works dictates what part of society the barrister is involved with, and therefore the people and problems the barrister will face and the expertise the barrister will develop.

CLERKS

A barristers' clerk, usually referred to simply as a 'clerk', might best be described as a cross between a personal assistant and a sports agent. Clerks' importance cannot be overstated. Solicitors contact clerks when they want to instruct a barrister. They may already know which barrister they want. If so, the clerk will check the barrister's diary and negotiate the barrister's fee. In other cases, the barrister the solicitor has in mind may be busy, or the solicitor may have a favourite barrister but that barrister may be too senior for the job, or the solicitor may not have a particular barrister in mind and may be contacting a particular chambers because of their general reputation, and the clerk must decide which of the barristers in chambers would be suitable and must try to 'sell' that barrister to the solicitor. Much of the work of a barrister in the first few years of **tenancy** (before the barrister has much of a reputation) is acquired in this way. Nowadays many chambers call their clerks **'practice managers'** and 'practice assistants'. Because clerks are shared by all the barristers in a set—and because of their important role in the development of barristers' careers—the clerks are the focus of the chambers and they steer the general reputation of the chambers.

 'Junior clerks', often teenagers in their first jobs who hope to become clerks, are on hand to carry files to court and to deliver documents and the like.

Clerks qualify by doing a set of exams and, while most started off as junior clerks, nowadays a few come in as graduates.

THE FOUR INNS OF COURT

There are four Inns of Court, all based in London: Gray's Inn, Lincoln's Inn, the Inner Temple and the Middle Temple. (Their full names are prefaced by 'Honourable Society of . . .', eg 'The Honourable Society of the Inner Temple'.) An Inn of Court, generally referred to just as an Inn, is a cross between a professional club and a guild. (A guild is a mediaeval trade association). When the Inns began, back in the thirteenth or fourteenth centuries, universities did not teach law (this began in the early nineteenth century) and there were no Bar schools to teach legal skills (until the Inns of Court School of Law was founded in the mid-nineteenth century), and these functions were therefore performed by the Inns.

Nowadays the importance of the Inns has greatly diminished. For students and pupils, the main significance of the Inns is that they are the principal providers of funding to **Bar school** students and, in addition, in order to become a barrister a person must **'dine'** at an Inn a certain number of times and then be **'called to the Bar'**, which involves going through a ceremonial granting of the status of **barrister-at-law**. (This is discussed further below in chapter nine). For **pupils** and **junior** barristers, the Inns also continue the compulsory **advocacy** training that the Bar schools started.

For London barristers, the Inns are also the physical setting in which their law world (in particular, their chambers) is situated. The Inns bear a remarkable resemblance to public schools and Oxford and Cambridge colleges, which all goes to make one sort of people feel immediately comfortable and another sort initially uncomfortable, but if you think of them as small villages then you will soon get used to them: it is nice to walk around and see familiar (hopefully friendly) faces. It also aids the barristers' sense of importance (or self-importance) to have a special bit of London that is only for them, and in which they can walk imperiously on their way to court.

Otherwise, for most barristers the Inns are very much in the background of practice, and play little part in their day-to-day lives. A minority of barristers are very active in the social communities of the Inns, and a much larger number use the Inns only for their law libraries and perhaps for the dining facilities.

LONDON AND THE CIRCUITS

About two thirds of barristers work in London, but that still leaves several thousand who don't. Historically a 'circuit' was a regional route that a judge would ride, dispensing justice from town or village to town or village. Nowadays, a circuit (sometimes called a 'region') is an association in which barristers in a particular geographic area can meet, and circuits perform some of the functions that the Inns perform for London barristers, such as a social community and training (although, as mentioned above, all barristers, whether in London or not, must also be a member of one of the four Inns of Court, which are all in London; further, London barristers are also entitled to be members of the South Eastern circuit). The circuits are: Northern, North Eastern, South Eastern, Midland, Western, and Wales & Chester, as well as the European circuit. In my experience, the smaller size of the circuits, as compared with the London Bar, means that generally they have more of a sense of community and more people get involved in social events than in the London Bar, notably at the rather boozy but fun circuit dinners that are held from time to time.

THE EMPLOYED BAR

As I explained above, about a fifth of barristers work at the Employed Bar. This does not mean that the other four fifths are unemployed; rather it means that those at the Employed Bar are not self-employed and do not work in chambers, but rather practise as barristers as employees within an organisation. These barristers still retain rights of audience in the higher courts, but are also allowed to do things that self-employed barristers may not do, such as taking statements and conducting correspondence on behalf of their client. (I should add that there are many employees who are qualified barristers but are not practising as such—in other words, they have changed career and become lecturers or businessmen or something else. These do not count as members of the Employed Bar.)

The principal employers who employ barristers are:

(i)   The government, through the Crown Prosecution Service (CPS).[5] The CPS prosecutes the vast majority of the criminal

---

[5] See http://www.cps.gov.uk/working/legaltraineeinfo.html.

cases heard in the courts of England and Wales, and employs about a quarter of all employed barristers. As well as taking in qualified barristers, the CPS does provide a small number of **pupillages** (usually six to ten per year), often sending pupils out for a month's placement in chambers. The CPS will not pay for the Bar Vocational Course (the **BVC** is a compulsory one-year course for all barristers, described in chapter eight) except as career development for those who were already employees of the CPS, and will only consider applicants who have finished the BVC and have their results and are ready to start pupillage immediately. The pupillage vacancies are ad hoc and will be advertised on the CPS website when they become available (contact the CPS to find out if any are likely in a particular year). See further the *Pupillages Handbook* (details under 'Applications' in the Further Information section at the end of the book).

(ii)   The government, through the Government Legal Service (GLS).[6] Most government departments employ GLS barristers, including the Department for Trade and Industry and the Revenue and Customs Department, with the biggest employing department being that of the Treasury Solicitor. As well as taking in qualified barristers, the GLS provides between three and six pupillages per year, usually sending its pupils out for a few months' placement in chambers. The usual time to apply is July two years before the pupillage is to start. The bad news is that this is nine months or so before you would have to apply to chambers. The good news is that if you get a pupillage then the GLS, unlike the CPS and chambers, will pay for your BVC and give you £5,000–£7,000 to live on for the BVC year (and sometimes will even pay for your **CPE**). See further the *Pupillages Handbook*.

(iii) Solicitors' firms, mainly employing barristers in their **litigation** department. Only a very few solicitors' firms actually provide pupillages; most firms that employ barristers take them in after the barristers have qualified at the self-employed Bar. Some law firms treat their barristers the same as self-employed barristers, with others treating them more as solicitors with extra advocacy and litigation skills.

(iv)   Local authorities. Most local government authorities employ barristers (and solicitors) in their legal departments but there are

---

[6] See http://www.gls.gov.uk.

very few pupillages offered. For more information contact the Bar Association for Local Government and the Public Service.[7]

(v) The Army Legal Service or Royal Air Force (recent advertising slogan: 'Fancy a job with a high flying law firm?'), where you would deal with courts martial (the military's internal criminal prosecutions), and general advice in war- and peace-time.[8] You must be a fully qualified barrister (or solicitor) before commissioning as an officer (ie the Forces do not offer pupillages).

(vi) Large industrial and commercial companies. Large companies often have their own legal departments and employ their own lawyers (solicitors and barristers) in-house. You are unlikely to get a pupillage in such an environment and will have to go in as a qualified barrister.

(vii) Newspapers and media organisations. As with industry and commerce, these employers take only qualified barristers and not pupils.

Many barristers turn to the Employed Bar because they have failed to gain a tenancy in a chambers they liked: going to work in a solicitors' firm is a good fall-back option for such barristers, who are often welcomed by the solicitors' firms because of the advocacy and litigation training that they have had. At least as many, however, choose the Employed Bar over the self-employed Bar because they prefer it, often for the following reasons:

- financial security while training to be a barrister: some employers, notably the GLS, will pay Bar Vocational Course fees plus a small grant.
- financial security as a barrister: employed barristers are paid a wage, with a pension, paid holidays and paid maternity/paternity leave. They may not make a fortune, particularly in government (although some employed barristers earn as much or more than self-employed barristers), but they won't starve or have cash-flow problems either.
- working as part of a team/department/division rather than on your own.
- the other trappings of employment: a cafeteria; a football team; secretarial support; often shorter, more regular hours, etc.

---

[7] See http://www.balgps.org.uk.
[8] See www.armylegal.co.uk and http://www.raf.mod.uk/legalservices. Unlike the Army and RAF, the Navy does not recruit lawyers from outside its ranks.

The Employed Bar is represented by its own **Specialist Bar association**, the Bar Association for Commerce, Finance and Industry.[9]

THE BAR COUNCIL AND BAR STANDARDS BOARD

The General Council of the Bar of England and Wales, usually known as the Bar Council, acts as the Bar's union, trade association, and guild and handles complaints against barristers (although, at the time of writing it is proposed that the Bar Council will be subject to the supervision and control of the Legal Services Board, a new statutory body). The solicitors' equivalent of the Bar Council is the **Law Society**. Since 2006, the regulation of barristers, which used to be carried out by the Bar Council, has been carried out by a new body called the Bar Standards Board (BSB), which is independent of the Bar Council and made up of a majority of non-barrister members. The Bar Standards Board has taken over from the Bar Council responsibility for the Code of Conduct, a code governing barristers' behaviour, and for qualification and pupillage and other similar areas, although some of the day-to-day administration of these areas is still handled through the Bar Council. If the Code of Conduct is breached then disciplinary action can be brought by the Bar Standards Board and ultimately the barrister can be **disbarred** by her or his Inn.

THE CODE OF CONDUCT, CONFIDENTIALITY, AND THE CAB RANK RULE

The Code of Conduct, referred to in the previous paragraph, sets out the obligations of a barrister, which include to '*promote and protect fearlessly and by all proper and lawful means the lay client's best interests*' and not to '*engage in conduct which is dishonest*'. This Code is important, is rightly emphasised during study of the BVC, and pervades the practice of barristers. Honesty and integrity are important in many spheres of life but particularly in the practice of the law, and especially in the largely self-employed world of the barrister, because barristers have only their own reputation and pride to rely on, with no

---

[9] See http://www.bacfi.org.

firm to hide behind or live off. Most judges were barristers and there-fore they know this and trust barristers to (for example) only present arguable cases, make allegations of fraud only with good evidence, and never to mislead the court. This helps the whole system to work.

Barristers are also trusted by their clients, and the law protects this trust. A barrister (or solicitor) cannot be made to tell the police or a court anything a client says to his or her barrister (in relevant circum-stances). This so-called 'legal professional privilege' exists to protect everyone's right to legal assistance by not deterring people from seek-ing and employing such assistance.

Further, there is a rule known as the **cab rank rule** whereby a barris-ter has a *'public obligation based on the paramount need for access to justice to act for any client in cases within their field of practice'*. This means that, like at a taxi cab rank, a barrister must take any client that comes his or her way. This does not mean that a barrister must take a case if it is outside his or her expertise, too hard or serious for his or her level of experience, or too lowly paid for his or her seniority, but it does mean that a barrister must not refuse a case because the barrister does not like the client or disapproves of what the client has done or is believed to have done. This rule is in place in order to ensure that all clients, no matter what they have done, can be represented by a bar-rister if they so wish.

I'M CONFUSED. DO I NEED TO KNOW ALL THIS?

Whilst you do need to have an understanding of the set-up of the Bar, including the Inns of Court, Bar Council and Bar Standards Board, circuits and Specialist Bar Associations, it is important to keep all of this in perspective. As you would expect, most barristers spend their working lives in their offices dealing with clients, paperwork, and emails, or in court presenting cases. The Bar Standards Board's Code of Conduct is an important moral backdrop to practice, and for Londoners the Inns of Court are the physical backdrop, but otherwise all of these institutions play a relatively small part in the everyday practice of the barrister (amounting to little more than a provider of the occasional lecture, advocacy course, or dinner). On the other hand, the difference between barristers and solicitors, the difference between self-employed barristers and those at the Employed Bar, and the idea of chambers and clerks, are all central to an understanding of what a barrister does and how he or she does it.

THE GUILTY MAN

The most common and annoying question the barrister or aspiring barrister is asked is 'how can you defend a man who you know is guilty?' This question, in this form, is inapt to what many barristers do (eg the non-criminal barrister might never 'defend' anyone who might be guilty but rather might try to prove that the contract was breached, the driver was careless, the mortgage was unpaid, etc) although its essence can be applied to their work also. The answer to the question is fairly revealing of what barristers do, and what type of mind barristers have, so here is my answer (although I am not a criminal barrister):

The 'objective truth', or 'what in fact happened', is irrelevant. Decisions are made by judges or juries on the basis of what has been proven to them to have happened such that they are sure ('beyond reasonable doubt'—the criminal standard of proof) or pretty sure ('on the balance of probabilities'—the civil standard of proof). The only relevant truth is what has been *proven* to the judge or jury *on the evidence*. The opinion of the barrister—in other words, what the barrister feels is proven—is irrelevant. The barrister's role is not that of investigator or judge, but rather the mouthpiece of the client. The burden is on the prosecutor to prove that the accused is guilty of the crime. Each client must, through his or her legal team, put forward evidence and argument as to what that evidence shows or proves, and the judge or jury then decides what has been proven. The court will never have all the possible evidence, so the accuracy of what was proven to the judge or jury is only as good as the process. The question 'what if you know your client is guilty' is meaningless: no one is guilty until proven guilty, that is, no one is guilty until after the court says they are, and whether they are guilty of a crime (or proven to have driven carelessly or not to have paid their mortgage) depends upon what is proven to the judge or jury and what the legal rules say about those facts that have been proven. As Samuel Johnson observes, one can never know a legal cause to be bad because

> you do not know it to be good or bad till the judge determines it . . . what you call knowing, a cause to be bad, must be from reasoning, must be from

supposing your arguments to be weak and inconclusive. But, Sir, that is not enough. An argument which does not convince yourself, may convince the Judge to whom you urge it; and if it does convince him, why, then, Sir, you are wrong, and he is right.

(James Boswell, *The Life of Samuel Johnson* (London, Henry Baldwin, 1791) para 24)

Indeed, there is more than a kernel of truth in Ambrose Bierce's joke definition of 'lawful' as 'compatible with the will of a judge having jurisdiction' (Ambrose Bierce, *The Devil's Dictionary* (New York, Albert & Charles Boni, 1911)).

The interesting question is, therefore, not 'how can you defend somebody who is guilty?' but rather 'what happens if a barrister knows something his or her client doesn't want to tell the court?' or 'what happens if a client wants a barrister to put a case that the barrister knows is untrue?'. Here the fact that a barrister has duties to the court not to lie, in addition to the duties to his or her client, becomes relevant. So the **Code of Conduct** provides that a barrister '*must not deceive or knowingly or recklessly mislead the Court*' and '*must not compromise his professional standards in order to please his client*'. The Code further provides that: '*the mere fact that a person charged with a crime has confessed to his counsel that he did commit the offence charged is no bar to that barrister appearing or continuing to appear in his defence, nor indeed does such a confession release the barrister from his imperative duty to do all that he honourably can for his client.*'

However, given what he or she knows, there are limits to what a barrister can honestly do. One thing the barrister is not obliged to do is to tell the court anything that the court does not know—the onus (the burden or responsibility) is on the other side to reveal the evidence against the guilty man. A barrister may object to the prosecutor's evidence and argue that that evidence is insufficient to prove the guilt of the client, but, as the Code sets out: '*it would be wrong to suggest that some other person had committed the offence charged, or to call any evidence which the barrister must know to be false having regard to the confession, such, for instance, as evidence in support of an alibi. In other words, a barrister must not (whether by calling the defendant or otherwise) set up an affirmative case inconsistent with the confession made to him*'. In other words, the barrister can keep the secret but cannot mislead the court. In practice, the barrister would be fighting with hands tied behind his or her back, and the client would often seek a new barrister.

RANKS OF BARRISTERS

There are three ranks of barrister:

1) **pupils** (also known as **pupil barristers**), who are not barristers but rather apprentice barristers;
2) **juniors** (also referred to simply as barristers), who make up the majority of all barristers (ie barristers of 15 years' experience are still 'juniors'); and
3) **silks**, the senior barristers who have attained the rank of **Queen's Counsel (QC)** or **King's Counsel (KC)** (or, within a team of barristers instructed on a particular case, the **leaders**).

A QC or KC is a barrister (or, more rarely, a **solicitor-advocate**)[10] honoured by special appointment by the monarch, although, in the light of recent reforms, this appointment now follows an application to an independent panel rather than, as used to occur, secret recommendations and nudges and winks. QCs and KCs (which term is used depends upon whether the reigning monarch is a queen or king) are entitled to wear a silk gown and are therefore also referred to as **silks**, with their becoming a QC usually referred to as **taking silk**. Generally it takes over 15, and often over 20, years before a barrister takes silk, and many barristers never do (for more about the process see www.qcapplications.org.uk). The first QC was Francis Bacon in the late sixteenth century, and nowadays about 10 per cent of barristers are QCs. Being a silk often opens barristers up to work that they did not get before, since many solicitors will not use a barrister for a certain size of case unless that barrister is a QC. However, this does not mean that the work floods in: often very successful senior **junior** barristers (ie senior barristers who are not yet QCs) take a cut in earnings when they become a silk because they move out of the area (in terms of types of case and work, not area of law) that they are well established in and have to break into a new sphere in which they are now the most junior practitioner but still very expensive.

When you become a barrister you are **called to the Bar** and your certificate will say that you are an **utter barrister**. The origin of this phrase appears to be the organisation of the halls of the Inns of Court, where there was a barrier or 'bar' separating the **masters of the Bench** or

---

[10] Two per cent of those awarded silk in 2006 were solicitors.

Benchers (senior barristers and judges, and a few others) from the rest of the hall. The outer, or 'utter', barristers were invited by Benchers to argue in moots and debates, and sat near the centre of the hall and further from the bar, whereas the more junior student barristers, known as inner barristers, sat nearer to the bar. Once utter barristers were permitted to plead in the law courts (after 1600), these phrases came to refer to the barrier in the law courts. Silks were permitted to plead within that barrier, whereas other qualified barristers (the utter barristers) were only permitted to plead outside the bar. Even today, in the higher courts the front row is reserved for silks, and other barristers must sit in the row behind. The term '**Bencher**' is still used in the Inns, but the phrases 'utter barrister' and 'inner barrister' are obsolete.

A word should be said about judges. In a career sense, judges are another senior rank of barrister. When a barrister becomes a senior junior or a silk, he or she often makes a choice as to whether to become a judge, the first step usually being to become a Recorder, who is a part-time judge who spends most of his or her time practising as a barrister as normal. Judicial ranks above Recorder are full-time posts, so sooner or later a barrister will have to decide whether to become a judge or whether to stay at the Bar. This decision turns on lifestyle (judges often have a shorter working week and longer holidays than barristers), money (most judges earn a fixed amount of between £100,000 and £130,000, which in many cases is far less than they could earn if they stayed at the Bar, although they get a good pension), and temperament (some people like arguing, some like deciding). It is important to realise, however, that becoming a judge is a very real option for many barristers and that, as explained above, because most judges were barristers (a few were **solicitor-advocates**) there is an understanding and empathy between the two that helps trials and other court hearings to run smoothly and fairly, and helps judges and barristers to mix well in the **Inns** and on **circuit** and elsewhere. Once they become judges, barristers are not allowed to remain as members of chambers (because of the need for judges to be and be seen to be independent), although they are often listed by chambers as former members.

PUPILLAGE

Before anyone is entitled to practise as a barrister he or she must complete a period of **pupillage**, which is essentially an apprenticeship.

Whether in the **Employed Bar** or **self-employed Bar**, a person will spend a total of one year as a full-time **pupil** under the tutelage and supervision of a **pupil supervisor** (who will be a **junior** barrister who has practised for at least six years). A pupillage can either be done in one go at one chambers, or divided into two periods of six months at two different chambers: the **first six** (or 'non-practising six months'), which must be completed in one continuous period, and the **second six** (or 'practising six months'), which can be interrupted by pauses of up to one month (although this is rare) and must be commenced within 12 months of completion of the first six.

A period of six or 12 months in a particular chambers or organisation will often itself be split into shorter periods spent with different pupil supervisors (eg three months with each pupil supervisor). Although in the majority of cases the entire 12 months of pupillage is spent in one or more chambers, a valid second six can include a period with a solicitor, an EU lawyer, a High Court judge, or other external training.

A pupillage is full time (over 35 hours per week) and cannot require more than 48 hours per week without the pupil signing a waiver (which is not unusual). A pupil must be given at least 20 days' holiday. Something to watch out for is that if a pupil takes more than five days of sick leave in any six-month period of pupillage the pupillage must be extended accordingly, and the Qualifications Committee of the Bar Standards Board must be notified.

As for what goes on in pupillage, that is discussed in later chapters.

WIGS, ROBES, AND OTHER FANCY DRESS

In the higher courts barristers must wear off-white ('salt and pepper' colour) horsehair wigs (although Sikh barristers are permitted to wear turbans instead). These wigs are usually kept in an oval lacquered wig case which is black with gold detail and which has the barrister's initials embossed on it. Judges wear their own style of wig (the 'bench' wig), and also have a longer wig for ceremonial occasions.

Barristers and judges also wear black gowns (known as robes) in court. As already mentioned, QCs and KCs wear a silk gown, and hence are referred to as 'silks', whereas other barristers wear what are referred to as 'stuff' gowns (meaning, according to the dictionary, that they are made of manufactured material or wool). The gowns have a little dangling piece of material at the back, on the end of which is a sort of pouch. It is often thought that this pouch existed so that the instructing solicitor could pay the barrister without the latter sullying himself by handling money, although in fact it seems more likely that the extra material and pouch is a vestigial remnant of what was once a hood.

A barrister carries the wig and robes in a drawstring bag of cotton damask (meaning a cotton silk mixture with intricate designs) embroidered with his or her initials. A junior counsel carries a blue bag and a senior counsel a red bag, although traditionally a QC or KC may award a red bag and the right to use it to a junior where the junior has given outstanding assistance on a case.

In courts (other than magistrates' courts), barristers wear a normal dark suit (with special jacket for QCs) but with **tunic shirts**, also known as **court shirts**, meaning collarless shirts worn with separate collars which are attached to the shirt by two collar studs (the studs operating much like cufflinks or split pins). When in court, the barrister will wear a wing collar (also worn by non-barristers for formal dress) attached to his or her court shirt; the colour of the collar will always be white, whatever the colour of the shirt itself. Also, instead of a tie, the barrister in court will wear **bands**, which are white rectangles of material that dangle from the neck (see illustration overleaf). Some say they symbolise Moses' tablets of stone. As with bow-ties, the hand-tied version of bands looks better than the elasticated version, and the so-called 'fused' version of the collar (the washable version) is better than the starched version (high maintenance) or the plastic version (which looks a bit cheap). In the office or in meetings a barrister will affix an ordinary collar to the court shirt and wear an ordinary tie, or even, in casual situations, wear no collar (in a style popularised by the Beatles and the past Indian Prime Minister Nehru). Female barristers may wear a wing collar and bands, or alternatively may wear a **collarette**, which is a soft collar with bands stitched on to it and a white fabric bib that sits under the jacket and covers the shirt or whatever is being worn underneath. A further alternative is a ladies' collar, which is the same as a collarette but without the bib.[11]

[11] The website of Ede and Ravenscroft, the legal and academic outfitters, is helpful in explaining shirts, collars, studs, and bands: http://edeandravenscroft.co.uk/Legal/FAQ.pasp. More information on wigs and gowns is available in Thomas Woodcock, *Legal Habits: A Brief Sartorial History of Wig, Robe and Gown* (London, Good Books, 2003), downloadable for free at http://www.edeandravenscroft.co.uk/Legal/images/site/Legal_Habits_book.pdf.

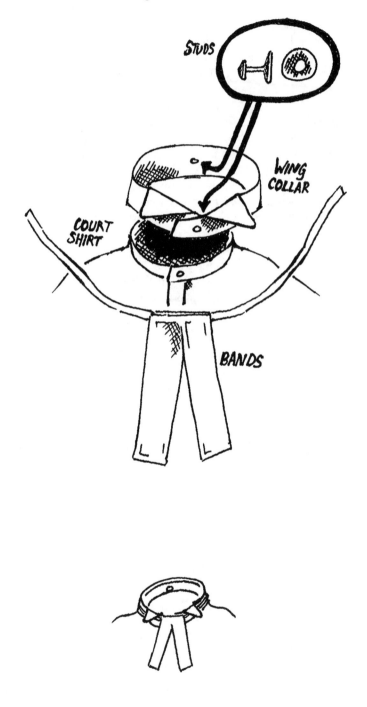

Solicitors (who, it must be remembered, can and do often appear in the lower courts) do not wear a wig or gown. **Solicitor-advocates** wear no wig but do wear a gown, albeit of a different type to that of barristers (indeed of a type that, some say, makes them look like court **ushers**). Unsurprisingly, many people argue that barristerial dress is anachronistic and should be abolished, although its defenders support it for giving a sense of importance to proceedings, and for conveying the idea that barristers are just representatives of the machinery of justice (and so should not be blamed or threatened for an unpopular outcome). Even those who support the wig and gown say, with some justification, that solicitor-advocates should have the same costume as barristers since they have the same rights in the courts.

HAND-SHAKES AND LEARNED FRIENDS

The Bar is a place of traditions, most of them fun and harmless. The fancy dress and terminology have already been referred to. Also, traditionally barristers do not shake hands with each other and do not carry briefcases to court, although these conventions have largely fallen away. One that has survived, however, is that barristers in court refer to each other as 'my learned friend' (as in: 'a moment ago my learned friend referred your Lordship to the case of *Donoghue and Stevenson* . . .')—and note that 'learned' is pronounced 'learn-ed'.

ACADEMIC SIDELINES

Because of the independent lifestyle of the Bar, and because some of the most legalistic points in litigation are often handled by barristers rather than solicitors, the Bar is naturally a more academic place than solicitors' firms are (although this applies less to City firms, and of course there are many exceptionally bright academic-leaning solicitors). A few barristers have come from a career lecturing in universities (I am one of them), but many more have no academic background and yet naturally find themselves involved in, and interested by, important points of law. It is therefore common for barristers to write legal articles in journals and to use their experience to write law books, which is also a good way of advertising their expertise to solicitors and other barristers. The author of the leading text on a particular area of law will usually be one of the leading **silks** practising in that field. Many barristers also give talks or seminars at solicitors' firms on recent legal developments or other legal topics, partly in order to drum up business from that solicitors' firm. This is in sharp contrast to a hundred or so years ago, when it was forbidden for barristers to write law books in their own name as to do so would amount to advertising, which was considered unsavoury and was therefore forbidden. This is why there are Victorian-era law books written anonymously, with the author listed as 'A Barrister'.

In addition to the many senior barristers who are also senior academics, there are senior academics who are not barristers but have strong links to a particular chambers. These academics cannot practise as barristers but can be called upon for their expertise when relevant legal issues arise, and are known as **door tenants** (as their name is on the door but they do not have rooms or practise in the chambers). Other door tenants include barristers practising in other regions or countries.

HOURS

Being in a service profession, if a barrister wants to keep his clients (ie solicitors) coming back for more, he often has to dance to the piper's tune. In any line of work it is difficult to predict in advance how long work is going to take, but this is even more difficult in **litigation** because unexpected tasks can arise in a case in which one is already instructed and those tasks usually have strict (court-imposed) deadlines: it may take longer than expected to draft witness statements, the trial timetable may move because of the unavailability of witnesses or judges, the Court of Appeal may grant permission to appeal (requiring you to draft the relevant documents immediately), etc. Sometimes a barrister can pass on work (particularly written work) to others by sub-contracting it to another barrister. This is called '**devilling**': a barrister pays another (usually more junior) barrister (the **devil**) to do the work and then the first barrister finishes it off and gives it to the client without the client ever knowing. Usually, however, a self-employed barrister who has a busy period is stuck with it because he is a one-man business and cannot pass the work on to a team of colleagues. Very early on most barristers make the horrible realisation that, because of these uncertainties, sometimes it will actually be impossible in the time available to do all the work that they have committed to. As one of John Buchan's characters observed:

> There is something about a barrister's spells of overwork which makes them different in kind from those of other callings. His duties are specific as to time and place. He must be in court at a certain hour. He must be ready to put, or reply to, an argument when he is called upon; he can postpone or rearrange his work only within the narrowest limits. He is a cog in an inexorable machine and must revolve with the rest of it. For myself I usually enter upon a period of extreme busyness with a certain lift of spirit, for there is a sporting interest in not being able to see your way through your work. But presently this goes, and I get into a mood of nervous irritation. It is easy enough to be a cart-horse, and it is easy enough to be a race horse, but it is difficult to be a cart-horse which is constantly being asked to take Grand National fences. One has to rise to hazards, but with each the take-off gets worse and the energy feebler. So at the close of such a spell I am in a wretched condition of soul and body—weary but without power to rest, and with a mind so stale that it sees no light or colour in anything. Even the end of the drudgery brings no stimulus. I feel that my form has been getting steadily poorer, and that virtue has gone out of me which I may never recapture.

(Buchan, *The Gap in the Curtain* (London, Hodder & Staughton, 1932) chapter 1)

Thus many barristers have unavoidable periods of very high levels of activity, working evenings and weekends preparing for the handling of witnesses on the next day of trial or simply doing reading and drafting work that won't fit into the working week. How often this occurs in your practice will depend upon how quickly you work, whether you are cautious in taking work on, and the type of work you do (since some areas of law provide fewer strict deadlines and less uncertainty than others). It should not be forgotten, however, that often after a bad period of work you will find the clouds clear and you have an almost-empty desk and then you can just take a week off to recover: you are self-employed and that's one of the compensations (although whether you do so or not depends upon various things including money and your **clerks'** dispositions). Nevertheless, it is common for barristers to do some work at the weekend (either at home or in chambers), and even if they are not doing so they will always carry around a mental list of the cases they are working on and the tasks to do. If you are work-shy or disorganised the Bar is not for you.

In addition, barristers are increasingly expected to be available to their clients (the solicitors) outside usual working hours. Many barristers have now followed the more widespread practice of solicitors and have 'blackberries' (hand-held mobile communication devices which receive emails wherever the holder happens to be). Even without blackberries, barristers can usually be contacted in an emergency (eg when a last-minute settlement offer has come through or an urgent court injunction is required) through their clerks, who are supposed to be available 24 hours a day if need be.

EARNINGS

As in all jobs, a barrister's earnings depend upon her or his seniority. The other major factor is the type of work the barrister does, above all because earnings depend upon who is paying. Barristers conducting criminal prosecutions are paid by the government, and most criminal defence work and a large proportion of family work is paid for by the legal aid system (ie the government again) rather than by the relevant individuals. The rates of pay for this work are set by the government rather than the market, and so, as governments have progressively tried to save money, the pay for publicly funded work has gradually got lower and lower (relative to other pay-scales) to the point where in 2005 there was talk of barristers going on strike because the pay was so low. A new barrister doing this sort of work may earn as little as £15,000–£20,000 per year, going up to £100,000 or more after 10 years, and up to, or more than, three times that as a silk. At the other end of the pay-scale, a new barrister doing commercial or tax work will probably earn £35,000–£90,000, going up to £300,000 or more after 10 years, and double that as a silk. A handful of top silks can charge £1,000 per hour.[12] As a result, if you walk around the Inns you will see more than a handful of sports cars. Other factors affecting earnings include the barrister's reputation (in other words, how good he or she is), how good the clerks are at getting the barrister work, whether his or her area of litigation is generally busy or quiet (since some areas are seasonal or dependent upon economic cycles), where he or she works (earnings in London are generally higher), and whether he or she is at the **Employed Bar** (earnings are generally lower than for those in self-employed practice).

---

[12] For more information on earnings see the tables on the Legal 500's website: http://www.legal500.com/l500/frames/barr_fr.htm.

These figures for the earnings of a self-employed barrister need adjustment before comparison with earnings by employees (whether employed barristers, solicitors, or anyone else) is possible. All earnings figures are quoted before income tax (at an average of, say, 30 per cent) and overheads such as travel expenses (unless the travel expenses are paid by the employer). However, barristers, being self-employed, have much higher overheads. As well as fixed set-up costs (a barrister, unlike a solicitor, has to buy his or her own desk, computer and books), there are significant ongoing running costs, such as office rent, stationery, photocopying and administrative support (secretaries and clerks). Solicitors and employees are provided all of these things for free, but barristers have to pay for them, usually by means of a fee to their chambers. Some chambers will charge a fixed minimum however much work you do, and some chambers will have a maximum, so that those earning the most pay proportionately less of their earnings, but most of the fee in most chambers is a percentage of earnings (before tax) in the region of 10–15 per cent. Clearly, this makes a significant difference to what you take home, so a barrister who is 'grossing' £100,000 will probably have under £50,000 to spend on his home and private life (after tax and chambers fees), whereas a solicitor with a wage of £100,000 will probably have more like £65,000 for his home and private life (after tax). This does not mean that barristers earn less than solicitors, since many barristers will have a gross income significantly higher than the earnings of comparable solicitors (at least until the solicitors become partners).[13]

In terms of how the earnings are billed, self-employed barristers often get paid by the hour, although for most hearings and trials, **clerks** will negotiate a fixed 'brief fee', and legal aid work is usually paid on a slightly different system which depends upon the number of witnesses and amount of evidence rather than the amount of time the work takes.

Whilst on the subject of earnings, it should be noted that many barristers do a few days a year of what is called **pro bono** work, which means work in the public good ('pro bono' stands for 'pro bono publico'), in other words work for free for those who can't afford to pay for it. Much of this is referred through the Citizens Advice Bureaux

---

[13] A commercial solicitor's starting salary (after the training contract) will be around £50,000, rising to in the region of £100,000–£120,000 after about 10 years, with partners' earnings significantly more than that (see www.rollonfriday.com). A non-commercial solicitor will start at between £15,000 and £20,000 per annum, going up to £35,000 to £70,000 after 10 years, and more than that once the solicitor becomes a partner.

and other such organisations, and since 1996 over a tenth of all barristers have done pro bono work through the charity named the **Bar Pro Bono Unit**.[14]

Finally, mention should be made of cash flow. Part of the order of things is that (for whatever reason) solicitors often wait until the **lay client** pays them before they pay barristers, and it will normally take between two and six months from when the work is finished (which may be months after the work is started) until the barrister is paid, and often pay won't come through until a year or two after the work has been done. The fees for publicly funded work similarly take a long time to come through. This means that while a new barrister will (hopefully) be earning a fair amount, he will often have several months with next to no actual income, while he waits for the lag time mentioned above to expire and for the fees to trickle in. Although some chambers will help with cash flow, generally a new tenant can expect to live on borrowings for three to six months (which adds up to a lot of money in rent and living costs). In my first few months I sometimes earned more in a day than I actually received in cheques in the whole month. This delay in payment will continue throughout your career, so you will always be owed a few months of pay. In effect you will work the first few months for free and never get paid for them until you retire or take extended leave (although actually it's the most recent few months for which, at any one time, you have not been paid).

INCLUSIVENESS AND DISCRIMINATION

In recent years the Bar has tried to throw off its image of a profession of white men, and it has had some success in doing so. One reason for the relatively low level of discrimination at the Bar is that barristers are very proud of their intellect and are fairly independent-minded and mature, and this tends to lead to a meritocracy and to exclude a laddish culture, which help to prevent the Bar succumbing to sexism, racism, or any other '-ism'.

Indeed, statistics show that the proportions of men and women becoming barristers are now approximately equal. This has not always been the case, and, ever since Ivy Williams was called in 1923

---

[14] See www.barprobono.org.uk.

as the first female barrister, the glass ceilings have continued to be broken year after year: Lady Hale was the first female appointed to the House of Lords in 2004, and Dame Rosalyn Higgins, a Brit, was the first female judge appointed to the International Court of Justice. However, the reader should not be under the impression that the 50:50 split that exists at the junior end is true of the Bar or bench in general: at the end of 2005, 67 per cent of all barristers, and 90 per cent of **silks** and higher court judges, were male. This does not indicate discrimination in the award of silk, rather an unequal division of applicants: in 2006 about 85 per cent of those applying for silk were male (which was the lowest proportion ever, and in fact the success rate for those women who did apply was higher than for the male applicants).

The ethnic spread throughout the Bar initially appears to be much less balanced, with the total proportion of those who do not describe themselves as white being 20 per cent of those in pupillage, 10 per cent of the Bar in total, and five per cent of those who applied for silk in 2006. These figures are fairly encouraging, given that the 2001 census data indicate that just eight per cent of the total population surveyed do not describe themselves as white.

If anything, the main area of lack of representation at the Bar is that of the poorer sectors of society. This is not the result of discrimination *per se*, rather it comes from the high costs of going to the Bar, namely the usual costs for any graduate profession (universities are expensive) plus the further costs of the **CPE** (where applicable), **BVC**, and **pupillage** years. There may also be some self-selection based upon a misunderstanding that the Bar is not for the poor, or a correct understanding that a large sector of the Bar are from middle class backgrounds.

MATERNITY LEAVE AND BABIES

As described in the previous section, it is clear that although around half of new barristers are women, this ratio is not found in the higher echelons of the profession. The reason why only some 10 per cent of silks are women is simple: babies. Many female barristers leave the profession when they have children, and many others return to work after several years but find that their time out, or their continuing maternal duties, prevent them from working enough hours as a barrister, or doing cases that are big enough, to get noticed and get silk (although these days one might think that this should equally be a problem for conscientious fathers).

Whatever your own approach will be, the key question is whether the Bar is better or worse than other professions if you want to have children. This is a difficult question to answer. In many ways the Bar is the ideal profession for those who want to have children, both in terms of long maternity or paternity leave and in terms of making time available to raise children. Barristers are self-employed and pretty well paid, so there is little to stop barristers deciding (and making it clear to their clerks) that they want to work fewer hours/days and therefore that they want fewer cases, or to stop them turning down the sort of cases that will screw up their family lives for a long time (ie long trials). As regards the cases a barrister does take on, it is generally up to the barrister when and where they put in the hours and do the work, so often they can make sure they are at home to tuck their children into bed or at school for parents' evening or sports day, if that is their priority.

However, despite all this, the first consideration, at least with regard to maternity/paternity leave, is money: as a self-employed person a barrister gets paid for what he or she does and so gets no paid maternity/paternity leave. Indeed barristers have ongoing expenses such as rent and chambers fees that carry on throughout maternity/paternity leave, although most chambers have a policy of letting barristers off a period of rent and expenses when they are on maternity/paternity leave (ie the other barristers pay the share of the person on leave). The **Bar Standards Board** recommends a period of six months' 'expenses holiday' for maternity leave, and one month for paternity leave[15] but, of course, there is little to stop a barrister with enough savings or other income taking longer. The second consideration is that in some cases the flexibility is to an extent illusory. Because of the uncertainty of litigation, there will often be unforeseen tasks and so barristers cannot guarantee that they will be able to leave their work at the office and come home at the same time every night. Further, part of most barristers' practice consists of trials, sometimes lasting weeks or even months and sometimes away from home, and during these periods of time working in the evenings and weekends is a fact of the barrister's life. If you don't do these cases you may find that your career progression is slowed, although becoming a **silk** is certainly not necessary for a happy or wealthy life.

---

[15] Pupils are also entitled to maternity leave but will have to apply to the Qualifications Committee of the Bar Standards Board if they wish to split their pupillage and to take more than 18 months to complete it.

CONTINUING PROFESSIONAL DEVELOPMENT

All barristers are required to do a programme of **Continuing Professional Development (CPD)**, which means that they must earn a certain number of CPD hours (or 'CPD points' as they are usually known) by going to or giving seminars, lectures, and other events that are accredited by the **Bar Standards Board**. The events are provided by the **Specialist Bar Associations**, as well as chambers, universities and companies. Writing articles, books, and chapters can also be accredited by the Bar Standards Board so as to earn the author CPD points. The Bar Council/Bar Standards Board keeps track of how many CPD hours you have completed.

New barristers are required to complete the 'New Practitioners' Programme', which means that they must complete 45 CPD hours in their first three years of practice (ie an average of 15 per year), of which at least nine must be advocacy training and at least three must be ethics training (see the Continuing Professional Development Regulations in Annex C of the **Code of Conduct**). All more senior barristers (including silks) must fulfil the 'Established Practitioners' Programme', which means that they must do 12 CPD hours per year.

A QUICK GUIDE TO LAW LONDON

While there are barristers and solicitors dotted all over England and Wales, with particular hubs in Manchester, Leeds, and Birmingham, the focus of the English and Welsh Bar lies within a couple of square miles in central London. It may be worth reading this section with a map or (see page 37), better still, taking a walk around to familiarise yourself with any parts with which you are not yet familiar.[16]

The Bar in London is dissected by Fleet Street/the Strand (two names for the same road) running east to west, and Chancery Lane and Gray's Inn Road running south to north. The centre of the London law world is the **Royal Courts of Justice (RCJ)**, the Victorian gothic building that looks like a Disney castle and sits on the north side of the Strand, near Temple tube station. This building is worth

---

[16] The Inner Temple website has useful and informative interactive maps of three of the Inns: http://www.innertemple.org.uk/tour/tour.html.

walking around, not only for the 'wow' factor but to get some familiarity with it for navigation purposes: the staircases and lack of direct connection between adjacent parts makes the experience not unlike a nightmare set in an MC Escher painting. The surreality is added to by the spa and gym in the basement ('the Wellbeing Centre') that was officially opened by Lord Chief Justice Woolf in 2003 for the exclusive use of judges, barristers, and RCJ staff, and the sporadic badminton playing that goes on in the main reception hall in the evenings (I kid you not).

Bordered by Fleet Street to its north, Blackfriars tube station to its east, the river to its south, and Temple tube station to its west, sits '**the Temple**', which contains two of the **Inns of Court**: Middle Temple to the west (with Middle Temple Lane running down it) and Inner Temple to the east (with a big car park in the middle of it). From the twelfth century until the early fourteenth century the Temple was the London base of the Knights of the Military Order of the Temple of Solomon in Jerusalem (the Knights Templar), a sort of police force that protected pilgrims on their pilgrimages and made a lot of money in the process (recently made famous by 'The Da Vinci Code'—some of the film was shot in the Temple); now it is mainly the home to barristers' chambers and the two Inns mentioned above.

To the north of the Royal Courts of Justice and to the west of Chancery Lane is Lincoln's Inn, another of the Inns of Court. On Chancery Lane sits the **Law Society** of England and Wales (the solicitors' professional body) as well as various legal outfitters and robe makers (the most famous of which is Ede & Ravenscroft[17]). If you head northward across High Holborn, the road that runs east to west roughly parallel to Fleet Street but to the north of Lincoln's Inn, you will come to Gray's Inn, the final of the four Inns, as well as the Inns of Court School of Law, the oldest of the providers of the **Bar Vocational Course**. The Old Bailey, the country's most famous criminal court, lies less than a mile off to the east of Gray's Inn.

Now for a word on the lawyers' drinking holes. There are various pubs and bars in law London and, unsurprisingly, they are filled to the gills with lawyers. A few of the key establishments are the following: of the Inns of Court bars, Middle Temple Bar (just off Middle Temple Lane at the south end, near the library) has the advantage of backing on to Middle Temple's serene gardens, although Pegasus Bar in Inner

---

[17] Joseph Webb Ede's robe-making business was founded in the seventeenth century, and Thomas Ravenscroft's wig-making business in the eighteenth.

Temple is slightly more swish and serves good food. On the Strand, El Vino's is good for wines and cubby-holes, The Old Bank is good for atmosphere and getting a table for a pub pie, and Daly's (on the corner of the Strand and Essex Street) is a popular destination after a victory or defeat in the **Royal Courts of Justice**. Behind the RCJ (ie sandwiched between the RCJ to the south and Lincoln's Inn to the north) sits the Seven Stars pub, which is a good eating and drinking establishment but very small—most customers drink their beer out on the lane if the evening is warm enough.

On High Holborn, The Cittie of Yorke is packed to its rafters and booths with barristers, particularly Gray's Inn diners, and serves cheap Samuel Smith's ale (although I would rate the decor more highly than the ale). The Bunghole is a more upmarket establishment with a good wine list and a nice cellar in which to sample it.

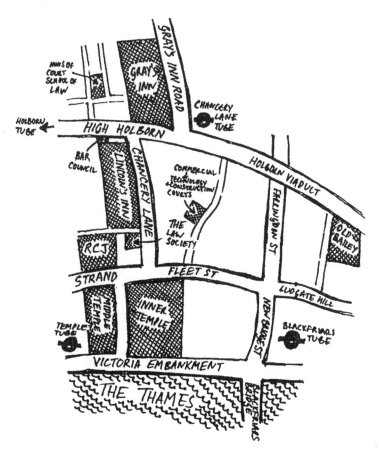

2

The Future of the Bar

As you will already have gathered, the Bar is hundreds of years old, and most of what I have described in the last chapter is how the Bar is and has been for a long time. However, this is not how the Bar will always be. Recent and imminent changes may dramatically alter things, and it wouldn't be fair for me to describe the Bar as it is without attempting to predict what you might be letting yourself in for in the future if you joined it.

SOLICITOR-ADVOCATES

The first dramatic change, mentioned above, is the breaking of the barrister's monopoly on appearing the higher courts. Since the Courts and Legal Services Act 1990, **solicitor-advocates** have also had these rights. There are about 3,300 such solicitor-advocates (a very small proportion of all solicitors), a large number of whom work for the **Crown Prosecution Service (CPS)** and for the government. Given that solicitors can now either conduct the higher court hearing themselves (if they are themselves solicitor-advocates) or use a solicitor-advocate within their firm, you might ask why they would bother to use barristers, and why more solicitors haven't become solicitor-advocates. The first thing that needs to be understood is that whereas barristers automatically have **higher rights of audience**, solicitors must do a further set of exams. Most solicitors will not do these exams (because of the fields they work in, or because, for whatever reason, they do not really want or have time to be advocates), and many of the people who would have wanted to do the exams became barristers in the first place or transfer from solicitors' firms to the Bar. Although some will be tempted to the financially safer world of the solicitors' firm, many prefer the independence and lifestyle that the Bar affords. More importantly, it is unlikely to be practical for solicitors to replace their use of barristers for higher hearings entirely (or even to use only employed barristers) for four main reasons:

(i) self-employed barristers are generally dramatically cheaper for the client (when comparing like-for-like seniority) because solicitors and their **firms** have much higher overheads than barristers (this doesn't mean that solicitors actually get paid more in wages than barristers earn, it means clients get charged more per hour by a solicitors' firm for a solicitor's time than by a barrister for his or her time);

(ii) workloads vary from week to week or month to month, particularly in **litigation**, so for a firm to have enough solicitor-advocates (or employed barristers) means that for much of the time some will be working below their full capacity, whereas self-employed barristers can be brought in for particular cases as required but need not be employed and paid all year round when litigation business is quieter;

(iii) it is often useful to be able to pass the risk of high-level mistakes on to self-employed barristers and their insurance policies, whereas if an employee makes the decision it is the solicitors' firm and its insurance policy that will bear the cost;

(iv) similarly, it is often useful to be able to pass the blame for tough decisions (eg 'if you go to court you will lose') to the self-employed barrister (for the same reason that companies hire in management consultants to sack people), and having self-employed barristers prevents the **lay client** leaving the solicitors and going for a second opinion, since in the barrister they already have a second and independent opinion.

The final consideration, which should not be overlooked, is that the majority of what barristers do (advice, drafting, lower court advocacy, **arbitration**) does not involve higher court advocacy. Solicitors are entitled to do all of these things and have been entitled to do so for a long time but, given that barristers seem to be busy enough, evidently solicitors still prefer to use barristers. This provides as good an indication as any of whether the introduction of solicitor-advocates is likely to spell the end of the Bar. (Further, it should not be forgotten that if the Bar did collapse or shrink, barristers would likely be welcomed with open arms by the solicitors' firms, so the stakes of betting on the Bar are not as high as you might think.)

DIRECT ACCESS

As described above, the barrister's monopoly on higher court advocacy has been broken. However, at a similar time, the solicitor's monopoly on handling clients was broken. There are now two schemes by which barristers can be instructed directly, without the use of a solicitor as intermediary. One is 'public access', under which any person may directly instruct a barrister if the barrister has done a particular Bar Council course. The importance of this should not be overstated: at the time of writing under 100 barristers (ie not that many) had qualified for public access. The second method is 'licensed access', by which licences to instruct barristers directly are granted to various organisations (although not individuals), usually organisations that have their own in-house legal expertise and so can do themselves what solicitors would otherwise do for them, such as some citizens advice bureaux, accountancy firms, banks, and hospitals, as well as various professional bodies that have been granted group licences. Both the Public Access Directory and the lists of licensed access licensees can be found on the Bar Council's website.[18]

These changes are certainly not revolutionising the way that barristers normally operate. Most clients and barristers still work through solicitors and are happy to do so, because there are certain tasks that barristers are not comfortable doing or do not wish to do. The current system of the split profession works well in the majority of cases, and direct access is, at least at present, little more than an exception to the general rule.

THE LEGAL SERVICES BILL

The most recent dramatic change is the general shake-up of legal service provision. Following the report of Sir David Clementi in 2004 (known as 'the Clementi Report'), the government has been planning

---

[18] http://www.barcouncil.org.uk.

a revamp of the way legal services are provided, its stated aim being to improve the situation for the consumers of these legal services by improving competition and service standards. The draft Legal Services Bill 2006 provides for 'alternative business structures' ('ABS'). Whereas at present there are strict rules on the make-up of solicitors' firms, henceforth, if (as seems likely) this part of the draft Bill becomes law, barristers and solicitors will be able to provide legal services from companies and partnerships that include other professionals who are providing other services (financial, IT, consultancy, etc). This may lead to solicitors' firms amalgamating with accountants and other financial firms but, for the same reasons why solicitor-advocacy is not likely to undermine the Bar, this is unlikely to have a large effect on the core of the Bar, although it may lead to renewed questions as to what distinguishes barristers from other legal practitioners.

PUPILLAGE AWARDS

Since 2003 there has been a minimum pupillage award of £10,000 that chambers must pay their pupils. The details of these awards are discussed below in chapter ten, but the significance for the Bar is twofold. First, this has increased many pupillage awards and so reduced the financial burden on entrants and therefore widened access by making the Bar more viable for poorer applicants (although there is more work to this end that is still to be done). The second effect is (like that of the introduction of any minimum wage) a one-off shrinkage in the number of pupillages, as each pupillage became more expensive for chambers. This latter effect makes the Bar more competitive overall, since there are fewer pupillages to go round, but it also makes pupillage itself less competitive, since there are likely to be fewer pupils competing for tenancy, and chambers will feel that they have invested more in each pupil and so may be more likely to keep them.

3

A Week in the Life of a Junior Barrister

In order to show what it is like to be a barrister, and in particular how it can vary depending upon the field a barrister practises in, I have asked several junior barristers (each with between one and five years of experience) to describe in their own words a typical week in their working life. Each summary is headed according to the field of the barrister's practice, and is preceded by a short description of the barrister's ethnic origin, gender, geographical area of practice, whether they are in chambers or employed practice, and their CV.[19]

A CHANCERY BARRISTER

(Mixed-race male in the first year of tenancy in a London chambers, with LSE undergraduate and UCL master's law degrees, having formerly lectured on trusts law part time for a year)

I have no typical working week. I have spent entire weeks working exclusively on one large case; on other occasions, I have spent weeks in chambers completing paperwork on several smaller matters. At the other extreme, I have had weeks where I have been in court every day; for example, I once appeared in court in Newcastle on Monday, Bedford on Tuesday, Guildford on Wednesday, before a registrar

---

[19] Although I have tried to get barristers from a variety of backgrounds, the sample is far from random because there are naturally similarities between my own background and those of the barristers that I know well enough to ask to contribute to this chapter.

in the High Court on Thursday, and Birkenhead on Friday. The only constant is that I have been busy since being taken on as a **tenant**.

There is a similar diversity in the types of matters that I advise upon. Over the past nine months, I have worked on commercial cases (advising on guarantees and on share sale agreements) and insolvency matters (such as disputing a liquidator's appointment), as well as dealing with more traditional **Chancery** fare. The more traditional work has included trusts (I have acted for a trustee of a large offshore trust), land (I have advised on two adverse possession claims, and, bizarrely, once on the law of allotments!), landlord and tenant (typically advising on lease renewal or dilapidations), and probate issues (such as the drafting of particular clauses in wills). The variety is wonderful in some respects—you feel that you are constantly learning about new areas of law. It is less good in others, as you don't generally charge for the considerable number of hours spent learning the law.

On average, I am in court about two or three times a week. I often appear for my clients in small applications (for instance, setting aside default judgments, applying for orders to enforce judgments, or appearing in case management hearings) or on small insolvency matters (sadly, I am very used to making people bankrupt). I have also appeared in about five trials, most of which have stemmed from the installation of dodgy double glazing! It is great to get into court and practise cross-examination in a relatively low-pressure environment **before** a district judge.

In contrast to junior tenants in a few of the large commercial sets, I don't do much **devilling**. I have probably devilled about six pieces of work in my 10 months of tenancy. I have, however, **been led** on quite a number of matters. Most recently, I appeared in the Court of Appeal, acting for a bankrupt whose trustee in bankruptcy was attempting to sell his family home; we set up the defence of limitation (which means that the other side took too long before suing) and succeeded in front of the judge. My **leader** very kindly let me follow his oral argument and respond to a Human Rights Act point argued by the other side; I spoke for only about fifteen minutes, but it was thrilling nonetheless. We are still awaiting judgment.

On other matters, I have been brought in as a **junior** at the pre-trial stage, to complete research and drafting. This is rewarding, as you get the benefit of discussing your work with a more senior barrister, which is something of a novelty at the Bar, as in the main your work is not checked—you are the expert adviser who your solicitors turn to when they have something particularly difficult or important, and the buck stops with you! Money-wise, I can't complain. I had a few lean months after I was first 'taken on', where I did quite a lot of work, but received next to nothing. More recently, the cheques have started to come in with greater regularity and I have paid off the initial costs of setting up a practice—such as buying furniture, a computer and printer, and a few essential books (*Chitty on Contracts* is terribly expensive). With regard to my workload, at times it is more manageable than at others. I worked very hard indeed during the first half of this year, with an eight-week period in February and March where I worked exhausting hours every day, including every weekend. This surfeit of work was caused by my becoming involved in a vastly complex case, but having to continue to serve my regular **instructing solicitors**. I am not complaining though. As barristers are self-employed, the simple rule is: 'if you don't work, you don't earn'. I think that most barristers would tell you that they would rather be too busy than too quiet.

So what am I going to do today? Well, I have some particulars of claim (the legal document setting out the details of a claim) to draft in a franchise dispute. I have got to make some amendments to a letter before action (a letter warning the other side that you are going to sue them unless they pay you) that I drafted last week as a result of further information being sent to me. And I have to prepare for a brief injunction hearing tomorrow, where I will attempt to have an aggressive individual barred from a particular local council's offices. Varied? Certainly. Interesting? Most definitely. I had better get cracking.

ANOTHER CHANCERY BARRISTER

(White male in the first year of tenancy in a Liverpool chambers, with LSE undergraduate and Oxford master's law degrees)

My week starts in the new Liverpool Civil Justice Centre appearing in the 'winders' list (a list of applications to wind up companies, almost always because the company is unable to pay its debts). This is a regular feature of my Monday mornings, and it's about the most straightforward work at the **Chancery** bar. Most applications are unopposed so the hearing is wholly procedural and usually very short, although some are opposed, and that is when it all becomes more interesting!

Most of my winders work is for out-of-town solicitors, because local solicitors tend to do this work themselves, which makes it a good opportunity to make contacts. The regularity of this work also means that you quite quickly get to know the local district judges. Usually I will be in court once or twice more during the week, spending the rest of the week working on papers. **Devilling** (or work for other barristers) is not really a feature of practice on the Northern Circuit, the **circuit** on which I practise. Although I also do some drafting of pleadings (formal court documents setting out claims and defences), most of my written work is advisory, covering a broad area of Chancery work. Common areas are beneficial interests in land; rights of way over land; agricultural and business tenancies; administration of estates; and the construction of wills. Most of the questions posed are new to me so my work often involves extensive reading and research before I write anything. I am fortunate still to share my supervisor's room, so I can discuss anything that concerns me before I send out my work.

This week I have a case on Wednesday and a heavy case on Friday so I restrict the amount of written work I do. I have to draft an **advice** on the construction of a will, which I take a look at, but the rest of my time will be spent preparing my court cases. Wednesday's case concerns an application for a third party debt order (an order against a person who owes money to someone who owes you money to pay the money directly to you). There is a dispute about whether the third party owes the sums claimed. Preparation involves reading and considering the witness statements and fairly extensive documentation. The **brief** for Wednesday comes in late so I am up into the early hours on Tuesday night preparing it. I usually prepare by setting out a chronology and noting down the key facts. I then make a brief note of any relevant legal provisions. I then prepare a fairly detailed note of the submissions I want to make. Judges have a habit of pulling you off the course you have mapped so it is fairly pointless writing out a full speech, but having a good note ensures that after being pulled off course you return to make the necessary points before you conclude your submissions.

On Wednesday morning I arrive in chambers just after eight to get some additional documentation faxed through and speak to the solicitor, and then I go down to Birkenhead County Court for the third party debt order hearing. The case goes well, and I am glad that I stayed up late! I speak with my **instructing solicitor** at court to let her know how the hearing went. I usually follow this up with an email setting out the terms of the order.

On Wednesday afternoon and Thursday I prepare my case for Friday. Friday's case is an application to strike out (ie have the court dismiss) a claim concerning a pension. I am acting for the pension trustees (the people administering the pension), and the case will be heard in the High Court in Manchester. I have already produced a **skeleton argument** (a written 'skeleton' of what my argument will be) that was sent to court and the other side last week, so much of the hard work has already been done. My instructing solicitors are a leading city firm in London. They have fully prepared the case, including a long witness statement and a large lever-arch file full of exhibits. The facts are numerous and complicated. The legal issues are also fairly involved, raising questions about jurisdiction and abuse of process. I look at some cases that may be of assistance, go over the documentation and facts, and prepare my submissions.

On Friday I am up early and travel over to Manchester. The hearing lasts all morning. The judge is probing in his questions and examines the case law and facts in considerable detail. This is the first time that I have done a full hearing in the High Court, so I am nervous, although I try not to show it. After final submissions in the afternoon, judgment is given. We are successful and the claim is struck out. I go for a drink with my opponent barrister afterwards and leave Manchester late afternoon, spending the weekend in the Yorkshire Dales with the junior members of my chambers. I manage to fit in a couple of runs on the hills and relax in the company of my colleagues.

A COMMERCIAL BARRISTER

(White male in the second year of tenancy at a London chambers, with Oxford undergraduate and McGill master's law degrees, having formerly lectured in law for a couple of years)

Monday sees me in the **RCJ** trying to kick someone out of their house. A man was made bankrupt as a result of not paying debts to his bank and others, and a person called a 'trustee' is then appointed to sell off the man's assets and pay the creditors from the proceeds. The trustee therefore has the bankrupt's rights to half of his house, and (through his solicitor) had **instructed** me to go and try to get an order for the sale of the house to raise some money. Over the course of a year of correspondence, the bankrupt argued that some of the debts had been paid off, and that his mother-in-law had a proprietary interest in the property. The dispute was factually fairly complex for this sort of case, so I prepared a written skeleton of my argument, which I lodged with the court on Friday so that the judge could read it before the hearing on Monday.

On Monday my **mini-pupil** and I strolled down to the RCJ. The bankrupt was represented by his brother-in-law, who was his solicitor, and in the waiting room he tried to raise some new matters with me. We then went into the judge's chambers (in this context, 'chambers' means a small court-room with no witness boxes) and argued the case. As sometimes happens, the judge hadn't read my written argument, so I had to present the whole thing orally, rather than just putting my main points. The solicitor on the other side then argued his case. He seemed to persuade the judge, but in my reply I argued quite forcefully that even if the bankrupt was right, there was still a substantial debt which he could not dispute and which would justify the possession order I was seeking. Time, however, was against me. The court listing office had allotted 15 minutes for the hearing, we'd already taken 30, and the judge had parties and lawyers from another case waiting outside. If we'd have had another 15 minutes I'm pretty sure I could have convinced him, but he didn't want to rush into a decision and in the end adjourned the matter until September, which will give the bankrupt a couple of months to try (and probably fail) to get evidence to dispute the debts. The solicitor on the other side and I went to the court listing office to arrange a date for the next hearing, and I had to telephone my **clerks** back at chambers because they keep my diary and only they know when I am free in September. We fixed a hearing and I and my mini-pupil walked back to chambers.

Back at chambers, I wrote a note of the hearing for the solicitors. I also sent an email to my clerks telling them what we decided about the hearing in September, and what hours I'd worked on the case. (Although the clerks had arranged a fixed fee for the hearing, and so the hours worked would not affect the amount billed, it is useful to have a record of work done so that the clerks know whether they are charging a high enough or too high a fixed fee.) I then went back to preparing for a trial that I have on Thursday involving a vintage car. My client had lent the car to the man on the other side and had only got it back several years later in a very damaged condition. The court had already determined that we were entitled to compensation, but there was to be a trial on Thursday on the amount of compensation, which would depend on whether, for example, the car had had some existing defects at the time it was being lent which later caused its engine to fail. I had to finalise the written skeleton argument, which I'd done some work on the week before, and prepare my questions for cross-examination of the defendant and the expert witnesses. However, on Monday afternoon another of my cases came back to me. This was an advice and draft defence I had done relating to a restraint of trade clause in an accountant's employment contract (a clause providing that he couldn't take customers or compete with his old employers for a year after leaving their employ). We represented the accountant, and our draft defence was due in on Wednesday. However, on Monday morning the solicitor rang to arrange a telephone conference on Monday afternoon with her and the accountant **lay client**. The conference lasted an hour or so, and mainly involved me asking questions of our client (not unlike the other side's barrister would do to him when in the witness box in court) and finding out that the facts were not quite as we had thought. I then spent that evening redrafting the defence so that I could send it to the solicitors first thing on Tuesday and give them some time to look at it before filing it on Wednesday.

Tuesday was principally spent preparing for Thursday's trial. Even at this late stage both sides kept coming up with new evidence and sending correspondence, so I had to have various telephone conversations with my **instructing solicitors** about what evidence needed to be disclosed and how to respond to the other side's latest letter. On Tuesday I also made a start on a short insurance advice that I needed to do. An insurance company had refused my client's insurance claim arising out of her car being stolen, so I had to advise on whether she had a case. This involved some criminal law, since there were questions as to whether as a matter of law the car was stolen (since it had apparently been stolen by the client's then boyfriend). After work I met my wife and we went into town to meet a friend who was in London on a short visit.

After mulling the insurance case over, I finished it off on Wednesday morning and sent it to the solicitors. I then spent the rest of Wednesday preparing for the trial the next day. I don't know anything about cars (I can drive but I don't have a car myself) and so it was a bit of a revelation having to learn about whether in a vintage car running a big-end bearing was likely to be caused by low oil pressure or aggressive driving. Part of the fun of the Bar is learning about obscure areas of the law and then asking experts questions as if you yourself are an expert.

On Thursday morning I went into chambers fairly early, printed out a couple of things, and then walked over to the solicitor's offices for a conference at half past eight. This was my first chance to meet the client and the witnesses so it was very useful to be able to find out what sorts of things they would be likely to say in the witness box, and whether they were likely to come across as honest and authoritative or shifty and bluffing. I also gave them the usual spiel about not trying to second-guess the questions and not trying to help the case, but rather just answering the questions honestly and concisely: all witnesses are nervous and think they are going to be out-manoeuvred by the barrister. They may be right, but it is not their job to be strategic—that is the job of the barrister on their side. We then went down to the Mayor's and City Court in central London in a taxi (keeping the receipt for tax purposes) and then, after we'd set up in the court and I'd put on my wig and gown in the robing room, we chatted and prepared. The trial itself was something of an anti-climax. The judge (quite rightly) thought that we should have settled the case and so before I'd spoken for five minutes he found a pretence to get us all to negotiate. The judge then left the court and after an hour or two of back-and-forth negotiation we managed to reach a settlement. The deal was good for us so I couldn't complain, although most of my preparation had ultimately been wasted. The barrister on other side and I drew up the settlement agreement and then got the judge back into court to approve it. My instructing solicitor and I then took our client and his witnesses for a pub lunch.

Back at chambers in the afternoon I saw that the solicitors had read my insurance advice and had agreed with my proposal to send a letter telling the other side of our claim. They asked me to draft the letter, so I got most of that done (although I was a bit woozy after a big lunch and a couple of pints) and then went home.

Of the 12 months I've been working, six months' worth was spent on about 65 small cases (about 20 hearings, and the rest giving advice and drafting pleadings), three months' worth was spent on one large insurance case, and one month's worth was spent on each of three other large cases (a fraud dispute, a construction dispute, and a financial services dispute). In the four big cases I've been led by a **silk**, and in the biggest one, the insurance one, I was led by a silk and another (more senior) **junior**. That case concerned tens of millions of pounds of losses in Hollywood film production, and our client, the insurance brokers, won at trial earlier in the year. The other side are now trying to appeal to the Court of Appeal and so we have to prepare our written response. As the most junior member of our team, the first stage of preparation of that response (including trawling through the transcripts of the trial) falls to me, and I'd agreed to have it done by next Tuesday. Friday, therefore, is spent trying to make headway on that. I take a break and have a sandwich on the lawns with a Bangladeshi friend from Bar school who is back in London to do some legal research.

Looking back on the week, I see I was in court twice. My average is probably one or one and a half days in court per week when I am not working on a big case, and then zero or five times a week when working on a big case (depending upon whether the case is a trial or not). Also, whereas these two hearings were in central London, at least half of my court appearances are outside or on the outskirts of London. Such hearings mean a lot more travelling time (not only on the trains, but also getting across London and allowing extra time for delays) but can be fun; wandering around Salisbury Cathedral and having fish and chips on the beach in Southend-on-Sea are recent highlights of how I've spent the hour immediately following two recent hearings in towns I'd never before visited.

The weekend then beckons. Leaving on Friday, I took a bit of the film finance insurance case home with me to do over the weekend. (I ended up doing one hour of leisurely reading in the sun on Saturday. On the one hand, it's a bit silly to break up a weekend for just one hour that you could fit into Monday. On the other hand, it's a fairly painless hour of extra work that you can bill for. I'm going through one of my dry patches money-wise: I've earned a fair amount but a lot of it is owed to me so my cash flow is not very good.) I also mentally recap what is coming up: part of being a self-employed barrister is being highly organised and constantly having a list of things to do in your head. On Monday next week we are expecting to get the supplemental argument from the other side in my big construction case, mentioned earlier: that, too, is going to the Court of Appeal, the hearing starting the following Monday. Monday and Tuesday next week will mostly be spent finishing the film finance work to hand over to my silk and the other junior on the case. Monday night is the annual chambers meeting at which we decide whether to give tenancy offers to our pupils, and I also have a drinks party to go to down in Inner Temple to celebrate one of our chambers' silks becoming a judge. I then have a couple of advices to get stuck into which I haven't opened yet, one concerning a dispute over a caravan, and another concerning a credit reference, and I then have to prepare for the construction appeal hearing. Never a dull moment if you like this sort of thing, and it turns out that I do indeed like it.

A COMMON LAW BARRISTER

(White male in the first year of tenancy at a London chambers following a **third six** *months' pupillage, after doing 12 months' pupillage at a commercial set, with a City University undergraduate law degree, having formerly run a recruitment company for a few years)*

The range of work that my chambers undertakes is very broad, and as a baby junior I am exposed to most areas within that range, which can involve commercial contracts, insurance, professional negligence, personal injury, road traffic and health and safety law, to name but a few.

There is an abundance of work and unless I am very firm with the clerks, ie beg, beg, and beg again for a day in chambers so as to work on papers, I find myself in court every day of the week. On average, I would say that I appear in county courts in and around central London on four of those days (with the occasional appearance in the RCJ), and in a court farther afield on the other day. I think that the most distant court that I have appeared in so far is Grimsby, but the idiosyncrasies of the train networks sometimes mean that a seemingly straightforward journey to a court in North Wales, for example, requires travelling to the town in question the night before if the matter is listed to be heard at 10 o'clock in the morning or thereabouts. The following is a record of a typical week's work.

Monday: an all-day trial in Barnet County Court, which inevitably required preparation on the Sunday. This involved a contractual dispute between a recruitment company and a cleaning company. One party maintained there was an oral variation to the contract, the other party denied this, so it was a straight dispute of fact which involved three witnesses on each side. I arrived back at chambers at 6 pm, had to settle an urgent defence that had to be filed the next day, finished that at 9 pm, and then resumed preparation for Tuesday's cases.

Tuesday: in the morning, a case management conference (a court hearing determining the future timetable and progress of the case) in a personal injury case, conducted over the telephone (these do take quite a bit of practice as they can be quite confusing and one does not want to be talking over the judge). Liability had properly been conceded by my client, the defendant landlord city council, and therefore the only issue to be decided was the quantum of damages. The claimant was quite seriously injured in the accident (probably in the region of £80,000–£85,000) and the main issue that had not been agreed was the amount of expert evidence that each party would be allowed to rely upon. In the afternoon, I finished some **devilling** for a senior member of chambers. This was an advice on liability in a contractual dispute between a provider of telecommunications equipment and an investment bank.

Wednesday: a trial in Oxford County Court listed to start at 11 am. Unfortunately, the case was not called on until 2 pm—this is not an uncommon occurrence and something that all junior members of the Bar become used to, but which **lay clients** are generally not used to, so it calls for some tactful diplomacy to ensure that they remain calm! I spent the journey back to chambers drafting a particulars of claim in an occupier's liability case between a child and his school. In the evening I attended a reception laid on by chambers for a city law firm. These marketing events are pretty regular and require a certain amount of background reading and mugging-up on the firm in question. They also require alternating between champagne and water!

Thursday: in the morning a small road traffic trial in Edmonton County Court. I was ready for action but my main witness did not attend to give evidence and all efforts to track him down came to nothing. My **instructing solicitors** instructed me to apply for an adjournment. As is often the case in these circumstances where no satisfactory explanation can be given for the absence of a witness, the judge refused the application and I was forced to proceed to argue the trial. Obviously, the chances of success are drastically reduced as a judge will attach only little weight to the written witness statement of a witness who has not turned up and so is not available for cross-examination by the other side. In the afternoon, I had an application to set aside a correctly entered default judgment in Guildford County Court. In the evening, I completed an advice on quantum in a personal injury case.

Friday: an all-day trial in Birmingham (this required an early train from Euston: a return ticket to Birmingham before 9 am is £168, after 9 am it is £36, so you do the maths!). This was an employer's liability case which required a lot of legal research beforehand. My instructing solicitor attended the trial and was a wonderful help throughout the day—not only in helping me find papers in the numerous bundles but her presence allowed me to concentrate more on the case itself rather than babysitting the witnesses before the hearing and during the lunchtime adjournment. The train journey back to London was spent reading a book (lovely), dozing (even better), and rallying myself for chambers' drinks in the evening.

Over the weekend I prepare a seminar that I am delivering on Monday for a law firm in Bristol, and look through the briefs I have received for next week. There are some weeks when I find myself working late during the week and coming into chambers at the weekend, and other weeks when I have a whole weekend off. Every junior barrister has the fear of not being busy and it is rare that there is exactly enough work for me to have a 'normal' working week.

The financial rewards are pretty decent, and one notices an increase in fees encouragingly regularly. However comforting it is to admire an impressive aged-debt though (ie the money I have earned and billed for but not yet been paid), I would rather actually have the money in my bank account. It is eternally frustrating how long certain law firms take to pay you, but a stream of reminders to the chambers' fees clerk is as aggressive as you can get if you want to be **briefed** again by that firm.

Life at the junior end of the civil/common law bar is challenging and rewarding. It is also tiring and unpredictable—I am fortunate to have some very understanding friends as I have lost count of the number of times that I have cancelled social plans at the last moment following a late brief.

A CRIMINAL/FAMILY/PRISON LAW BARRISTER

(White female in the fifth year of tenancy at a Southampton chambers, with Exeter undergraduate and McGill master's law degrees)

I am a provincial barrister of five years' **call** practising on the Western Circuit. That basically means that my work is focused in courts around the Southern region: Bournemouth, Southampton, Winchester, Portsmouth, and Bristol, with trips approximately once every month to the **Royal Courts of Justice** or the Principal Registry in London for High Court work. I am a tenant in a general common law set where junior **tenants** are encouraged to have a broad practice in more than one area of law before they go on to specialise in their chosen areas after they are at least five years' call. My practice reflects that philosophy. Now, at five years' call, I practise in all areas of family law (ancillary relief, care work, and private family law), crime, and prison law. My week started on Sunday with a chambers meeting at 9.30 am at a conference room in a local hotel. As a set we are now too big to have full chambers meetings in chambers itself. I wasn't happy about having a meeting so early on a sunny and hot Sunday morning, but as I am still fairly junior and there are controversial items on the agenda, I felt I had to attend. To be fair, the issues were bigger than usual: we are moving to new premises and have to choose a new name and discuss the construction plans and budget. We also debated (again) the chambers charges scheme: all tenants in chambers pay the same fixed rent and then a fixed percentage of what they earn. The junior tenants want more of a levy and less of a fixed rent, and the senior tenants the opposite. The debate rages on past midday before the meeting finally ends at lunchtime and I can have a few spare hours before I have to start preparing for Monday's case: a family law final hearing in an intractable contact and residence dispute.

In the end, I can only bring myself to do three hours of preparation work on Sunday evening before going to bed. I am representing the father who seeks 'residence' of the two children (ie wants to be their full-time carer). The mother currently has residence of the children and is not allowing the father contact. I read through the trial bundle making preparation notes and then draft a chronology (a list of relevant dates and events) and short case summary for the judge before calling it a day at about 11 pm.

On Monday morning I get up early (at 5 am) to finish my case preparation. I plan a short opening speech setting out the background to the case, and my cross-examination of the mother and the CAFCASS officer (court welfare reporter) who has interviewed the children and prepared an independent report and recommendations of what is in the children's best interests. I set off up the M3 in my car at 8 am and arrive in time for my conference with client and solicitor at Aldershot County Court at 9 am. I have met my client at previous hearings and we get on well so we can immediately talk comfortably about all the aspects of the case.

I warn my client that the children have suffered their parents' acrimonious separation and are now settled with the mother and that therefore the court is very unlikely to give him residence. The real issue, I explain, is how to obtain a regular pattern of contact between the children and their father. The CAFCASS officer recommends that the mother retain residence and the father get contact every Wednesday after school and on alternate weekends from Friday after school to Sunday evening. My client accepts the recommendation of the CAFCASS officer, agreeing that he will not pursue his application for residence as long as the mother agrees to the level of contact recommended. If the mother will agree to contact then a deal can be reached, but if not then the father will pursue his application for residence at a full hearing in order that he can play a meaningful part in the children's lives. My opponent in this case is a very experienced circuit practitioner whom I know well. He is clearly having difficulties convincing his client to promote or facilitate contact between the children and their father. Eventually, after much negotiation, a tentative agreement is reached on most of the issues. The only issue between the parties is whether the father should have staying contact (ie where the children stay over) on alternate weekends for two nights from Friday to Sunday or just one night from Saturday to Sunday. Negotiations go on all morning. The mother will not agree to staying contact on Friday nights.

My opponent and I **appear** before the circuit judge who is waiting patiently in the hope that matters might be settled, avoiding the need for a hearing. We apprise the judge of the progress and it is decided that there should be an abbreviated hearing on the single issue of whether the children's staying contact should be for one night or two. Having heard evidence from the CAFCASS officer and submissions from both **counsel**, the judge gives a short judgment stating that for the first two months there should be staying contact for just one night on alternate weekends, but then building to two nights with their father in accordance with the CAFCASS recommendation. My client is happy. My opponent and I draft the residence and contact order giving effect to what was agreed and ordered, and get the judge to approve it. We also agree that at the appointed time the father will drop off and pick up the children from the bottom of the driveway with the mother staying in the house, because whenever the parents meet they have explosive rows and the children should not be put through this.

It is 3 pm when I eventually leave court and start driving back to chambers in heavy traffic. At chambers I check emails and empty my pigeon-hole of papers and new cases that have come in that day. I check what the new cases are about by quickly reading each **brief** to ensure that nothing urgent is required, before filing them away ready for each hearing. I write a short attendance note summarising the hearing that day and fax it to my instructing solicitors along with a copy of the draft order. Now it is 6.30 pm and I can start thinking about tomorrow's case. On Tuesday I am scheduled to do a prison law case in Wales. I am instructed to represent a prisoner serving a life term for a murder he committed 17 years ago. Tomorrow is his parole board hearing and he is applying for release into the community on life licence. I have already read the case papers (when they came into chambers one week ago) which, as is usual in these cases, consist of a 'dossier' of reports on the prisoner compiled by the Parole Board. They include the Secretary of State's views (from the Home Office), psychiatric reports, probation reports, psychology reports, and various prison progress reports from professionals who have come into contact with the prisoner throughout his prison 'career'. I reread the dossier and make notes. The case is fairly straightforward and it is only the prison psychologist who opposes this prisoner's release, saying that he should remain in open prison for a further period of testing before release should be contemplated. At the hearing I will be required to cross-examine the prison psychologist as well as question the Home Probation Officer and the Prison Probation Officer. My room-mate (I share a room with one other barrister who is a few years more senior than me) is also in chambers doing paperwork, and a number of colleagues come into the room and chat about the day they have had. Eventually I finish work and leave chambers at 8 pm.

Because of the long journey to Wales, I get up on Tuesday at 5 am and am on the road driving by 5.45 am. The hearing starts at 11 am but I need to have a fairly lengthy conference with the client because I learn from the paperwork and my **instructing solicitor** that the client is of below-average intelligence and therefore requires matters to be explained very fully and very slowly. I prefer to get to my destination with plenty of time to spare rather than have to rush or panic when I get delayed in heavy traffic, so I usually set off unnecessarily early and then stop for breakfast and read through my case papers when I am close to my destination. I drive to Wales, go over the Severn Bridge and stop at a service station for breakfast where I do another hour and a half of work before driving on to the prison. I go through security and meet with my client and discuss his case with him. I go through all of the contentious dossier reports and explain areas that will be points of concern for the parole panel. This is his fourth parole board hearing of an application for release: he already knows the procedure.

There are three parole hearings listed before the Board that day. We are the second case. The first runs over time so we have to wait until 12.30 pm before our hearing commences. The Parole Panel consists of a circuit judge as the chair of the panel, a consultant forensic psychiatrist, and a 'lay' member who is usually extremely experienced in prison law issues.

The hearing starts with my application, and then the Lifer Governor reads out the Secretary of State's view opposing release. I question my client and lead him through his evidence before the panel and then they ask him questions on his offence, his attitude, and his progress within the prison system. Some of the questions and answers are very graphic indeed, and I am not sure that the Panel will be too impressed with all of my client's answers. The probation officers and prison psychologist give evidence, and the panel and I ask them questions. In particular, I cross-examine the prison psychologist for about 45 minutes and then I make a closing speech in support of immediate release upon life licence. The entire hearing lasts for three and a half hours with a short half-hour break for lunch (the prison provides lunch for the panel but unfortunately not for the advocates). As is usual, the judge then states that the panel will consider their evidence and notify us of their decision within seven days, and I have short conference with my client to make sure he understands everything that happened. It is extremely difficult to predict the outcome of parole board hearings, so I always avoid giving any sort of false sense of security in that respect. I wish him the very best of luck with the result and he is very grateful for my efforts.

I leave the prison at 5 pm and start the long drive back home in rush-hour traffic. I am starving, not having had any lunch, so I stop for some food at another service station before pressing on home. I am anxious to get back so that I can start preparing for Wednesday's case which is ancillary relief (finances on divorce). The case was originally given to one of my colleagues in chambers, but she has had to pass it to me because she has another hearing that clashes with it. While I am at the service station I telephone my instructing solicitors in my prison case and give them feedback on the hearing. I then phone my clerks. I am told that, in fact, my colleague is now free tomorrow and I am not therefore doing the ancillary relief case after all. This means that I am not in court, so I will be doing paperwork, billing and generally catching up with things. I may even have time to go to the gym that I am still paying an extortionate membership fee for. I am so relieved! By the time I get home I am fit to drop and certainly too tired for the gym.

Wednesday is spent in chambers. There is little point in fighting through rush-hour traffic just to get there, so I make the most of my day out of court and have a leisurely morning, getting up at 8 am and making my way to chambers for 9.30 am. There is nothing to stop me from simply working at home today if I want to, but all of the case papers I need to work on are in my room in chambers and I find it more sociable to work there. Checking all 48 emails and fielding calls from solicitors with various different queries on cases in which I am instructed on takes most of the morning. Today's main task is to write an advice on a complicated High Court family case about removal of children from England to Ghana. After about half an hour of research I get dragged (not very reluctantly) off to lunch to the local sandwich bar with my chambers colleagues. The rest of the day is spent researching my advice, save for a phone call from one of my regular and very loyal instructing solicitors, asking for some on-the-spot (free) advice on a care case that she has, which I do my best to help her with. She assures me that I will be **instructed** when the case comes up for hearing.

Tomorrow I am representing a wife at a directions appointment (not the final hearing) in ancillary relief proceedings. I have two lever-arch files of financial documents to read through in preparation for the hearing, which is listed at Bournemouth County Court at 2 pm, so fortunately I have the whole of Thursday morning to prepare for the case. I decide to go home and I finish off my written advice (on the Ghana case) there after dinner.

On Thursday morning I get up at 6 am and work from home. I plough through my brief in the ancillary relief case (those two files). I make short summary notes as I go, condensing all of the information and creating a Schedule of Assets to send to my opponent and give to the judge at the hearing. The husband has a high-powered profes-sional job and lives with his girlfriend; the wife works part time and lives in the former matrimonial home with the three children (aged 9, 12, and 14). The case is only listed for a half-hour directions hearing, but it is hoped that a settlement can be achieved with some careful negotiation. I arrive at court at 1 pm in time for a conference with my client (whom I have not yet met) and my instructing solicitor, with whom I have become good friends over the years that I have been in practice. My client is very nervous so I do my best to calm her nerves and explain that today's hearing is simply a directions hearing to identify the key issues, facilitate negotiation, and set down what is to happen before the main financial dispute resolution hearing. We don't have enough information to negotiate properly (can the wife take over the mortgage? what is the value of the property and the amount of mortgage still owing? etc). My opponent is a local solicitor. He is adamant that there should be an immediate sale of the property, as his client wants money to rehouse now (he is currently renting). However, the wife (my client), who desperately wants to stay in the house, cannot take more work without getting childcare and cutting her tax credits, and she would then be financially no better off. We appear before the district judge sitting in chambers, and I set out the relevant issues and each party's positions. A directions order is made to gather information (ordering that a surveyor be instructed and the parties give each other the necessary information). The case is relisted (ie a new hearing is put in the court's diary) for the financial dispute resolution hearing in four weeks' time. I drive home at 4.30 pm, stopping at chambers on the way to write a short attendance note on today's hearing and pick up my papers for tomorrow.

On Friday I have a conference in chambers on a particularly acrimonious ancillary relief case involving a large number of properties. The wife has been my client for about four years, in injunction proceedings arising out of domestic violence, and proceedings concerning residence of and contact with the children. Now she is arguing that property investments which are really the husband's are being held in her husband's father's name, and that her husband has also secreted money away from the joint account over the years in shares that he has not disclosed. The paperwork is voluminous and I have spent hours trawling through everything. The client attends the conference with her solicitor. We have a lot to talk about. My client has legal aid funding to run her case and I therefore have a professional duty to the Legal Aid Board to advise them that the public funding should be stopped or limited if the funded client has less than a 50 per cent chance of success. I therefore need documentary and other evidence to support each allegation. We spend three hours from 4 pm looking for a paper trail of bank transactions which might prove that a number of the properties were in fact purchased with matrimonial money, and therefore the wife has what is called a beneficial interest in them. By the end of the conference it is my view that my client cannot establish a strong enough case with regard to six of the nine relevant properties of her husband's father, and therefore I must advise the Legal Aid Board of this. This makes a huge difference to the amount of assets potentially involved in the case that the parties will be able to argue over, and my client is understandably very disappointed, but accepts my advice. We then go on to discuss making an offer to the husband and his father to settle the case, and I am instructed to draft an offer letter that can be served on the other side within seven days. By 7 pm I am exhausted and extremely glad that it is the weekend.

A PROPERTY AND COMMERCIAL BARRISTER

(White female in the fourth year of tenancy at a London chambers, with a Cardiff University undergraduate law with German degree)

It is difficult for me to set out the contents of my typical working week as my weeks can vary so considerably. The only thing that can be said is that each week is typically busy! The nature of my practice is such that each week generally involves at least one court appearance. Occasionally I am in court every day of the week, but this is becoming increasingly rare and my time is now more evenly distributed between paperwork and court hearings than it was when I started my tenancy.

The beginning of last week involved **devilling** some papers for a more senior property **tenant** who was attempting to meet all of his deadlines before going on holiday. Devilling only forms a small part of my practice these days, as I tend to be heavily involved in running my own cases or carrying out work on the two cases in which I am being **led** by senior members of chambers.

I was given the devilling at the beginning of Monday and told that it had to be forwarded to the barrister whose case it was in sufficient time for it to be checked by him and sent out on or before Wednesday morning. The case involved drafting an **advice** on the merits of tenants bringing various claims against their landlord. I spent the majority of the day carrying out the relevant research and wrote the advice during the evening. Having proof-read the advice with fresh eyes on the Tuesday morning, I forwarded it to the other barrister. He then rewrote it slightly in his own style and forwarded me a copy for my reference. It is always encouraging to see minimal changes in the version which is actually sent out to the solicitors.

The rest of Tuesday was spent on other paperwork and preparation for cases due to come up later in the week. I was in the Principal Registry of the Family Division (a family law court) on the Wednesday afternoon in order to obtain a final charging order over a judgment debtor's property. I am not a family practitioner and I had never appeared in the Principal Registry before. However, this was a favour for a solicitor for whom I do a considerable amount of property work and was a straightforward application in which there were no specific family rules applicable. Nevertheless, I felt strangely like a duck out of water!

Prior to attending that hearing on Wednesday I had spent the morning finalising the **skeleton argument** I had started on Tuesday for a half-day trial which was due to be heard in Newcastle on the Thursday afternoon. The case was not complicated, but involved a wide range of financial regulation statutory provisions with which the court might not necessarily have been familiar. Consequently, I wanted to set out those provisions in some detail and provide the court with an opportunity to consider them by faxing over my skeleton argument prior to the hearing.

I caught a relatively early train to Newcastle on Thursday morning and was due to arrive at just after midday, leaving sufficient time to get to the court for my 2 pm trial. I thought that I had built in adequate time for the train to be delayed; however, I was not expecting any delay to be over an hour and a half. There is very little you can do in such circumstances: you have to telephone the clerks to inform the court you will be late, and get a message passed on to any client you may have waiting, then just sit tight and keep willing the train to move. I finally arrived at court at just after 2 pm to find that the court was running late in any event. I did not get in **before** the judge until 2.45 pm, and then the matter was adjourned for 28 days as my solicitors had failed to send out witness statements to the correct address. So, I'll have to do the journey all over again in a few weeks time. Very frustrating but not uncommon.

The trip back to London consisted of preparation for my hearing for the following day in Portsmouth, which was another three-hour trial. This time I was acting for a computer course provider. We were (ie my client was) being sued by a former student for recovery of his course fees. There was a vast amount of factual information which had to be marshalled in order to prepare my cross-examination of the other side's three witnesses. The other party was not represented but conducted the case himself, and the matter ended up lasting most of the day before the judge gave judgment in our favour.

I spent the day in chambers on the Sunday because I knew there was paperwork I needed to catch up on, having been out of chambers for most of Thursday and Friday. I had received instructions on the Thursday morning to settle a skeleton argument in relation to an appeal, with the argument due to be sent to the court on Monday morning. Unfortunately, it transpired that, having considered the papers on the Sunday, there was simply no arguable legal basis for my client to defend the appeal; consequently, I was not in a position to draft a skeleton argument. Therefore, instead, I spent most of Sunday writing the solicitors a note of advice setting out the reasons why I could not do what they wanted me to do!

A PUBLIC LAW AND EMPLOYMENT LAW BARRISTER

(White female in the first year of tenancy at a London chambers, with Cambridge undergraduate and Harvard master's law degrees)

On average I am probably in court about once or twice a week, with the nature of the work I am doing varying considerably from week to week: my chambers does employment and public law although, at least to start with, I got more employment than public law work because there is more employment work that is suitable for very junior barristers. About half of my cases are on my own, being **led** by a more senior barrister on the other half. **Devilling** is rare for me and becoming rarer as my own caseload increases.

On Monday I prepare for a case management discussion (CMD) in a disability discrimination and unfair dismissal case. CMDs are interim hearings in employment cases, where the parties' representatives get together with a Chairman of the Employment Tribunal to clarify the issues in the case and to set directions as to how the case should proceed. Whilst CMDs tend to be fairly informal and cannot result in the final determination of any of the substantive issues in the case, it is important to be on top of the papers and clear about your case, because otherwise you risk making unwise concessions or missing crucial points. I read the papers, taking a note of the key events as I go along and tabbing up the file with post-it notes so I can find my way around it easily. I then prepare a list of the issues in the case, some suggested directions, and also amend the pleadings (drafted at an earlier stage by my solicitor) to clarify our case. I send these over to the barrister on the other side, and he calls me with a few things he wants added to the list of issues and some comments on the directions. He is very reasonable and we manage to agree everything fairly quickly.

A defence has come in from the other side in a pregnancy discrimination case I'm doing, so I go through that and then ring my solicitor for a quick chat about it. I also catch up with some billing—sending my clerks a list of the periods of time I have spent on various cases so they can send out invoices to the solicitors. I try to keep a record of all the time I spend on things and update my clerks regularly, but it's easy to let this slip when I'm very busy. At some point I will have to sort out my VAT and tax returns—another task that always falls to the bottom of the list.

On Tuesday I get in early and go through the other side's documents list in a sex discrimination case I'm doing, checking which of their documents I haven't already got and need to request. This would ordinarily be the solicitor's job but my solicitor is acting **pro bono** and basically as a 'post box' (something she neglected to mention when I agreed to take the case on) so I have to do quite a lot of the day-to-day running of the case. It is pretty common as a junior barrister to be instructed to do work that would usually be done by a solicitor, because this usually works out cheaper for the client.

I then have a long telephone conference call with another barrister in chambers and two solicitors in relation to some education cases we are working on together. The junior solicitor and I went to visit the clients last week to get information from them and give some preliminary advice, and we report back to the other members of the team and discuss what needs to be done next. The four of us are working on a whole raft of cases together and know each other well so the call is very informal. We agree that the solicitors will prepare draft letters warning the recipient of a claim to come (which is a lucky escape for me as this could easily have been my job). We need to get the letters off very quickly as the school term is about to end, and, if we decide to proceed, we will need to issue the judicial review claims challenging the relevant decisions in time to get an urgent hearing before the start of the next school year. Urgent deadlines are very common in public law work because judicial review proceedings have to be brought within a very short time of the decision being challenged (three months at the most), and because the cases are usually being brought to stop or change an ongoing situation or to prevent something happening, rather than simply to get compensation for a past event. This means an unpredictable workload and some late nights, but it is also exciting and means you get to see real changes being made to people's lives as a result of the work you are doing.

A defamation point has cropped up in relation to one of the education clients about the capacity of a body to bring an action for defamation. I do some research and have a chat with a colleague who specialises in media law, and prepare a short note of advice for the solicitors, and a draft paragraph to be inserted into a letter. Then I look back over the papers for tomorrow's hearing.

In the evening, I prepare a set of instructions for an educational psychologist in relation to a special educational needs case I am doing. The local education authority has decided not to assess my client's child to see whether he should be classified as having special needs, and my client is appealing to the Special Educational Needs Tribunal to try and reverse that decision. I had read the papers over the weekend to get a grip on the nature of the child's difficulties at school, so I look over my notes and also remind myself of the relevant legal test in the statutory code of practice, before drafting a short introduction to the background of the case and a set of questions for the expert, trying to ensure that she covers everything we need her to deal with. Not having a great deal of experience in instructing experts, I ask a more senior colleague in chambers to cast his eye over the final product. I often seek the advice of people in chambers, and have found that they are always happy to help, no doubt remembering their own first few years in practice.

On Wednesday I go to Reading Employment Tribunal for the CMD for which I did the preparation on Monday. The chair of the tribunal, who is about to go on holiday, is extremely pleased that we have agreed everything and done all the work for her. She approves all our suggestions, so the hearing goes very smoothly.

On my return to the office I write a note for my solicitor setting out what happened at the hearing. It is very common as a junior barrister to be in court on your own without a solicitor. Writing an attendance note not only helps the solicitor, it also covers your back should there be any later dispute as to what happened. My solicitor asks me to prepare an advice on the merits of the case, which I happily agree to as I have already done much of the necessary reading when preparing for the CMD. My solicitor has already spoken to my practice team to discuss fees for the advice. As the client is paying for the case himself and is of fairly limited means, the fee will probably be fixed at a fairly modest level, taking into account my estimate of the length of time it will take me to complete the advice. I almost invariably spend more time on a piece of work than I end up billing for, particularly because I often have to carry out a good deal of research as the points are ones which I have not come across before. This cannot really be factored into the fee, as if I was more experienced the same level of research would not be necessary. My workload is extremely varied so I am not doing the same sorts of cases day in, day out. This means I have to work harder and bill for less, but I regard it as a fair trade-off for interesting and diverse work, and as I become more experienced in more areas this will become less of a problem.

While I've been out a fax has arrived with the latest correspondence from the other side in a community care case I'm doing about an investigation into abuse at a residential care home. This is a case that I worked on as a **pupil** last summer with another member of chambers, but she was unavailable when further matters arose so the solicitor instructed me to do the case on my own. I get quite a lot of my work through links with solicitors I worked with as a pupil, and through recommendations from other members of chambers. The local authority has agreed to reconsider its report as a result of our representations, and my solicitor wants me to look over a letter she has written setting out the changes we think are necessary. I look back at the advice I wrote a few weeks earlier, to check that she has covered everything, and give her a quick call to let her know that the letter is fine.

I spend the rest of the afternoon preparing for a talk I am giving that evening to a group of education solicitors about some of the provisions in the government's recent Education Bill. The provisions are extremely complicated and I always find it hard to concentrate if I've been in court earlier in the day. Luckily the seminar session is meant to be very informal, so I can justifiably produce a fairly broad summary of the key concepts in the proposals as the basis for discussion, without going into great detail. I manage this with seconds to spare, and the talk appears to be fairly well received. I will try to convert the brief paper into a more detailed article for one of the education law journals. Writing articles is a good way to get your name recognised by solicitors, and also means you know a subject really well should you then be instructed in a case involving that subject. Finding the time to produce such articles in the midst of court and solicitor deadlines is another matter.

On Thursday I spend most of the day working on an environmental case I am involved in as a junior to another member of chambers. We have just lost in the Court of Appeal and we are applying for permission to appeal to the House of Lords. I reread the judgment and the submissions of the other parties on permission to appeal and costs, have a quick chat with my leader about our approach, and then draft our reply to their submissions. This is quite a short document, but because the case was extremely factually and legally complicated, and because I was brought in only at a fairly late stage, it takes me a long time to remind myself of the history of the litigation and to look up all the references I need. By the end I am drowning in a sea of papers and in need of a break, so I arrange to meet a friend for coffee in the gardens of the **Inn**.

The afternoon is spent reading the skeleton arguments and witness evidence in another case in which I am a junior—this time a judicial review of a decision to close a school. This case is publicly funded and there is only sufficient funding for one barrister, so I am technically **devilling**—the work will be billed as done by my leader, the fees will go him, and he will then pay me. Unlike with traditional devilling arrangements, however, the solicitors know that I am involved, and my name is on all the pleadings and skeleton argument. This is great, because it means that I build up a reputation with the solicitors, and also that my name will go on the judgment, which is likely to be reported in the law reports. There are issues with the funding because our solicitors are in dispute with the Legal Services Commission (LSC) as to the level of 'community contribution' our clients must pay towards the cost of bringing the case. Our clients will not be able to raise the level the LSC says they must raise, so if we lose the case and the LSC does not change its mind then we may only get half of our fees. This is one of the many hazards of doing publicly funded work. Some (but not much!) of my work is privately funded and paid at a decent hourly rate, and this helps to keep my earnings at a reasonable level. Of course, I haven't seen half of the money I've earned this year yet, because it can take months, if not years, for fees to come in. Luckily my chambers give me an interest-free loan which is paid monthly, so I don't have to worry about not being able to pay my rent etc. When fees come in I pay them over to chambers to pay off the loan.

In the early evening we have a general meeting in chambers to discuss various matters relating to recruitment of new members, changes to the building, and the administration of chambers. I am on the management committee and buildings committee in chambers so I have to go to a fair few meetings, but I like having an input into the running of chambers, and the meetings are sometimes a welcome break from bashing my head against the brick wall of some difficult legal issue.

On Friday I get an urgent call from the clerks asking me to go down to the **RCJ** because, although the barrister in charge of the particular immigration/ human rights case cannot go to court today, the court has unexpectedly failed to take the case out of its diary. Luckily I have a suit in the office so I get changed, grab some papers from the clerks, and run down to court, which gives me a few minutes to read the relevant order and the correspondence, and to find the barrister on the other side. It seems there is no problem with the consent order itself: it simply has not been registered by the court. This is something of a relief as I am not sufficiently up to speed on the case to argue about substantive issues. Upon explaining everything to the judge, it transpires that there was an administrative error in the court listing office.

On my return, I put together an index for the authorities bundle for the education judicial review. Preparing bundles of authorities is a dull and time-consuming task which invariably falls to the most junior barrister. Today I am in luck as our administrative team has time to collect some of the materials and do the photocopying for me. I always feel guilty about offloading such onerous tasks onto the staff, and promise to buy them beers to make up for it. Some papers come in for another CMD in a disability discrimination case. Although the CMD isn't until next Friday, I asked for the papers this week because I will be in court hearings on Wednesday and Thursday and preparing for it on Tuesday. If there is anything difficult in the case for Friday I would rather know now so I can gauge how much time I need to set aside to prepare it. I read the papers, noting down the chronology of events as I go in order to save time later. The issues for the CMD appear to be quite narrow—a fight about the disclosure of medical records and the instruction of a joint expert. I print off some relevant cases and take them and a textbook with me to read over the weekend, before escaping to the pub with some friends from work.

A TAX BARRISTER

(White male in the fifth year of tenancy at a London chambers, with Oxford undergraduate and master's law degrees, having formerly spent less than a year as an accountant)

I've been asked to write about a typical week to give an idea of what life at the tax Bar is like. It might perhaps help to make some headline points at the outset.

First, tax is all about questions of law. Although the facts must be ascertained at the outset, the issue is how the statute applies to those facts, which involves questions of statutory interpretation. In contrast, in criminal law, for example, it is typical for everyone to know and agree what amounts to the crime, with the question being whether the accused committed it. Similarly, in commercial law, very often the issue is to find the facts and determine whether they amount to a breach of contract. Tax law raises points of law like no other area. Secondly, our tax code is both vast and complicated and even senior practitioners do not carry it all around in their heads. So, almost every piece of work will involve some legal research. The more experienced you get the less work will be required and the quicker it will be accomplished (the definition of intelligence is knowing where to look things up!), but as tax law is constantly changing this remains central to practice at the tax Bar. So, if you enjoyed studying law then tax might well appeal to you. If what turns you on is the thought of getting stuck into witnesses on cross-examination, then you're probably better off elsewhere.

Thirdly, the majority of the work at the tax Bar is advisory. In other words, the issue is essentially always: 'What are the tax consequences of doing X and can any charges be avoided by doing something else?'. This is really a question of problem-solving and is what most of us spend most of our time doing. The other major type of work is contentious tax work. Most often this involves disputes between HM Revenue & Customs ('HMRC') and taxpayers, which relates to the regulation of an important clash between the rights of the citizen and those of the (increasingly cash-strapped) State. As in other areas of law, these disputes may be settled before reaching court, and most of us appear before the courts and appeal **tribunals** less frequently than in other areas of the Bar. However, when cases do arise they will often raise interesting points of law.

Fourthly, don't be misled into thinking that tax is a narrow area. Anyone with money or economic activity may be subject to tax, and in the four years plus that I've been in practice I have advised multinational conglomerates, well-known plcs, large and small private companies, partnerships, charities, trusts, and many individuals from all backgrounds. I have also litigated both for and against HMRC. UK taxes include income tax, capital gains tax, corporation tax, inheritance tax, VAT, stamp duty, stamp duty land tax, and national insurance. I frequently advise on all these taxes. In addition, the answer to a tax problem often involves issues of contract, trusts, land law, and EU law, so a good grounding in these is a big help. Finally, tax lawyers need a good grasp of commerce because solutions need to be workable in the real world.

On Monday I arrive in chambers and, after the inevitable checking of the emails, my first job is to check and sign out an **opinion** which I sent to the clients in draft by email the week before. This is easier said than done as it is lengthy and concerns the tax aspects of a proposed property development. Recently I've been doing a lot of commercial property work, which has been generated following a book I wrote on stamp duty land tax when that was introduced in 2003.[20]

My next job is to write a quick note summarising a conference and agreeing some documentation—again this concerns a residential development—and I am advising on stamp duty land tax with one of my chambers' QCs doing the VAT. Incidentally, I very rarely do junior work (ie **led** by a more senior barrister): I appeared as junior in the Court of Appeal whilst still a pupil; and in the four and half years since then I have done one advisory piece of work as junior and two joint conferences (this being one).

Finally, I prepare for a telephone conversation the following morning. One of my regular clients wants a quick chat to discuss creating an offshore unit trust as a vehicle for holding investment property. Tuesday morning we have the chat and the solicitors go off to talk to the clients, as there may be some commercial obstacles to overcome.

The rest of Tuesday is spent on a piece of tax litigation on which I have been advising, on and off, for the last couple of years. One issue has settled but HMRC are, in essence, now trying to obtain information from the client's accountants. HMRC has very wide information-seeking powers and the only way to appeal is by way of judicial review, but my job is to draft a letter to HMRC resisting the request. To do this job well I need to read quickly the ten or so cases where the courts have considered this, although doing so, sadly but predictably, fails to yield a killer point, or much that I didn't know already.

On Wednesday I'm instructed for a conference at 9.30 the following morning. Electronic communications mean that everything has to be turned around increasingly fast. The client is a charity and the issue is chiefly the availability of income tax relief (also known as 'Gift Aid') on various types of donation. This is a good example of an area where I understand the structure of what is going on but am going into the details (and the devil is there, of course) for the first time, and so it means that I have to work a little later than I otherwise would have done. One of the frustrating aspects of our tax system is that frequently finding the answer can take a couple of minutes but checking

---

[20] Michael Thomas, *Stamp Duty Land Tax* (Cambridge, CUP, 2003).

it much longer. As a barrister I am responsible for both the initial research and the final signing out of the work, in contrast to my previous employment in a large accountancy practice where these responsibilities would be divided up. The responsibility to get things right is a serious burden as it is all too easy to miss a point and clients will sue if things go wrong.

The conference takes up most of Thursday morning. Conference is my favourite method of advising both because I get to meet all kinds of people and because you can explore the ground much faster and the clients get the chance to explain things which were not immediately apparent from the papers.

Thursday afternoon I finish off the draft letter from HMRC that I started on Tuesday. Friday morning I consider a set of papers on stamp duty land tax concerning lease extensions on a block of residential flats; I will advise by telephone and email on the following Monday. I work from home on Friday as it saves the commuting time, and I have the books available electronically. Finally, I consider a set of papers that arrived Thursday night for a telephone conference on Monday morning; again it is a property tax question and the **instructing solicitors** are in this case also the **lay clients**.

Someone once wrote a series of books entitled 'The good thing about . . .'; I would say that the good things about the tax Bar are the interesting nature of the work and the challenge of solving the legal problems which it poses, thereby helping businesses to function. The variety of situations I am asked to advise on ensures that the work is never dull, although the complexity of the tax system does mean that sometimes the time required to be spent to do the work properly is disproportionate to the tax at stake; this is a real concern for our tax system. The opportunity to defend the rights of individuals against the might of a government bureaucracy is also attractive. Finally, the fact my diary is not in general dictated by court hearings means that although I work very hard, at least I have more control over my life than I would in many other areas of the Bar or as a solicitor. This is invaluable to me as I have a young family.

A FOREIGN AND COMMONWEALTH OFFICE-EMPLOYED BARRISTER

(White male in the third year at the Foreign and Commonwealth Office (FCO), with Exeter undergraduate and McGill master's law degrees, having done pupillage at a London chambers and had a stint as a judicial assistant in the Court of Appeal)

One of the biggest differences that I have noticed from life at the **self-employed Bar** is the structure of an average work day. I am currently based in London, just off Whitehall, and arrive at work anywhere between 8 and 9.30 in the morning, depending on the amount of work or energy that I may have on a particular day. In the evenings, when I have no meetings or receptions to attend, I tend to leave the office between 5 pm and 7 pm. Other colleagues, especially those with families, have made arrangements to job-share or work from home for part of the week.

Each assistant legal adviser at the FCO is given certain departments to advise—these departments may cover geographical areas (such as the Middle East and North African Department) or may deal with particular themed issues (such as the Human Rights, Democracy and Governance). I advise the Iraq Policy Unit, the Sanctions team, and the Global Business Group.

I start my Monday morning by reading reports that our embassies from across the world have sent in over the weekend. One or two are from our embassy in Baghdad and as a legal adviser to the Iraq Unit I pay particular attention to these reports. Fortunately none give rise to any legal questions and I spend the rest of the day reading and answering emails. I have emails from all of the departments that I am advising at the moment. Unless something is particularly urgent I try to group my emails by department so that there is a theme to the work that I do. I can be asked to advise on issues that touch upon a vast range of legal fields, from domestic law surrounding human rights or data protection to public international or European law, so anything that provides a theme to the work is helpful.

I start off by dealing with emails from the Global Business Group— I have been asked to draft an agreement with an international organisation for a position that the UK government has agreed to fund for three years. However, I am given no clear idea of what the department wants the agreement to include so I suggest a meeting later that afternoon, via telephone or video link, at a time that is convenient for relevant colleagues in London and New York to attend. The next email contains a new draft of a treaty sent through to us by a foreign government and I am asked for comments. It is an International Promotion and Protection Agreement (or a bilateral investment treaty, as most other countries call them) and the new draft contains some novel proposals, so I spend the next hour or two involved in some research in our legal library and consulting other legal advisers who have advised on the drafting of these agreements before me. And so the day carries on—either trying to catch up on old emails or dealing with new ones that may arrive. Sometimes I am just asked to read over a document and confirm that it does not give rise to any particular concerns; other times I am asked to provide specific advice on legal issues that may impact upon a proposed policy initiative.

I try, if possible, to take lunch away from my desk. I probably succeed about half the time. On Monday I grab a sandwich and return to carry on ploughing through the emails that have mounted up over the morning. I am conscious that my week in the office will be a short one as I leave mid-afternoon on Thursday for a conference in Paris. Because of this I am anxious to ensure that I stay on top of my work

In the same vein I arrive quite early to work on Tuesday to prepare for a meeting with a Foreign Office minister later that morning. The meeting concerns a consular case of a British national detained abroad. There is a long history to the case that I need to review and I have to be prepared to advise on questions of what the UK government can and cannot do to assist.

I finish the meeting in time for my weekly French lesson. I have not had an opportunity to complete the homework set the week before so I'm a step behind the rest of the class from the outset. Although we can have intensive language training before we head off for a posting abroad, we are required to have (or work towards having) a reasonable level of French at all times, hence the weekly French lessons for all legal advisers.

I return to my office with a sandwich and spend the afternoon drafting a letter to Treasury Solicitors who are acting for the government in a High Court case concerning Iraq. The case has given me an opportunity to work with lawyers from across Whitehall and provides a taste of the varied careers that are available at the **Employed Bar**, just within the government. I am able to respond to a few further emails and leave the office in time to attend a lecture at the International Law Association on terrorism and international law. Ongoing legal education is something that is encouraged—either

through voluntary attendance at evening lectures or through attendance on longer courses ranging from one day to two weeks.
The remainder of my week in London is occupied with attending
meetings or, the electronic equivalent, reading and answering emails.
I do find time on Thursday morning to fill out some of the paperwork
that is a necessary evil of the job. I complete two expense forms for
trips to Libya, Paris, and Brighton last month and I even manage to
complete a section of my annual appraisal form. There may be no tax
returns to do at the Employed Bar, but being part of a large organisation brings its own paperwork!

I am left with time on Thursday to have lunch with friends from the
office before heading to Waterloo station and the Eurostar to Paris. I
am on the trip with a colleague from the Global Business Group and
we are heading over for a conference on Friday at the Organisation
for Economic Cooperation and Development. We have one meeting
scheduled over dinner with staff from the British Embassy on the
Thursday evening. Friday is spent listening to experts talking about
developments in the field of investment treaties. As usual with such
conferences, the opportunity to speak to our counterparts from
across the world during the coffee breaks is as important as the conference itself. My small talk has had to improve. We manage to have
some particularly useful exchanges with representatives from
Mexico, Germany, and the European Commission. One outcome is a
likely trip to Mexico City in a couple of months, certainly preferable
to discussions in an overcast London.

My week finishes with a drinks reception at the conference; a reception that also marks the start of an extended weekend that I plan to
spend with a friend who is studying in Paris . . .

A CITY FIRM-EMPLOYED COMMERCIAL BARRISTER

*(White male in the third year of practice in the advocacy team of
London law firm, with an Oxford undergraduate history degree and a
Graduate Diploma in Law from City University, having done pupillage
at a commercial chambers in London)*

My role varies from case to case. If I am heavily involved in a case,
it often makes sense for me to carry out tasks that would otherwise

be carried out by a solicitor. At the moment I am working on a claim against a firm of auditors (ie accountants) and a number of directors brought by our client, the receiver of a company. The company became insolvent due to losses caused by the rogue trading of one of its employees. The receiver's job is to try and get in as much money as possible to pay off the company's debts. Our case is that the auditors should have spotted the trading and the directors should have put a stop to it, so they are both responsible for the losses. I first became involved when I was pulled in to help draft witness statements in preparation for the trial. This meant several trips up and down the country last summer to interview potential witnesses. Since then, the claim has been stayed (which means temporarily put on hold) whilst the parties try to reach a compromise through mediation (a structured form of negotiation where the parties appoint a mediator whose role is to facilitate a deal). I attended the mediation, and had the pleasure of putting together a settlement agreement on the hoof between our client and one of the other parties. I also produced notes on various legal issues as part of our preparation for the mediation. Today I am drafting a letter of advice to our client setting out the issues it needs to consider. I will then discuss my draft with the partner in charge of the case and amend the letter to incorporate her comments.

On another case, I am playing the traditional role of a barrister. Our client says it is owed a sum of money under a guarantee given to it by a Dutch company. Unfortunately, there is an error in the guarantee document which appears to release the Dutch company from any liability to our client. We have brought proceedings to have the mistake rectified. I advised our client on the merits of its claim and have since drafted the pleadings (the documents in which you set out your case). In all of this I was supervised by a partner. I produce the documents, and he and I talk them through before they go out. Unless it is totally mundane, a partner is supposed to sign off on everything that is sent out. In principle, therefore, final responsibility rests with someone else. However, there is still pressure on me since I am the one who should know the case back-to-front and who is supposed to have considered the legal issues in detail. We are gearing up for the trial of the claim, and at some point this week I need to produce a draft of our **skeleton argument** for the hearing. The actual trial will be conducted by one of the senior barristers in our team, so he will provide input into the skeleton argument before it is finalised.

At any one time I am usually involved in one large case, as well as a couple of smaller cases. This happens naturally: if I am busy on a large case I won't have much time to devote to other matters, so will only get involved with smaller cases. Additionally, about 30 per cent of my time is spent producing notes of advice on discrete legal issues. Often these will lead to a greater involvement in a new matter.

We try and handle as much work in-house as possible, but sometimes it is sensible to get a second opinion from a more senior barrister or a barrister with a particular specialism from the self-employed Bar. We also use barristers from outside the firm for trials. We have a couple of senior barristers in our advocacy team, but they cannot work on every matter. So, like a **junior** in a chambers, I occasionally work as a junior for barristers who don't work where I work.

The frequency with which I go to court varies hugely. Sometimes I will go several months without going near a judge; at others it will feel like my entire working life is spent preparing submissions for court. Since I work in-house, I tend to get involved in cases at an earlier stage, often well before there is even the prospect of a hearing on the horizon. The percentage of cases that I work on which end up in the court is therefore lower than if I was at the self-employed bar.

Although most of my work comes from within my department (the litigation department), I also get work from other departments in the firm. For example, a solicitor in the corporate department might ring up and ask if I can review a clause in a contract that they are drafting or talk through a particular issue, and give an opinion on whether it will work in practice. It is rare that I give an answer off the top of my head. I usually need to think about it and do a bit of research before emailing them my thoughts. If it's a tricky question, I usually discuss my thoughts with a partner in my department before sending anything off.

Whoever I am doing the work for, I have to make sure that I do the best that I can. I rely on the solicitors in my firm for my work, and if they don't think that I am a safe pair of hands, they will ask someone else—be it one of my colleagues or a barrister at the self-employed bar. Unlike my friends in chambers, all my instructions come from one firm (the one I work for). If I get a reputation for being slapdash or unreliable, people won't come to me and I will end up missing out on the interesting cases or without enough work to keep me busy. Since I am on a salary I get paid whether I am busy or not, but we are supposed to record all our time, and have minimum targets that we are supposed to meet. Additionally, bonuses are calculated based on the hours you have recorded over the previous 12 months, so there is an incentive to take on work and to keep busy.

The billing targets are not that difficult to meet. I usually aim to get in to work before 9 am, and I tend to leave the office at any time between 6.30 pm and 8 pm. I work later than 8 pm fairly infrequently—usually if I am preparing for a hearing. Between 9.30 am and 5.30 pm there is a fair amount of people traffic: secretaries, trainee solicitors, paralegals, library staff, and other lawyers, so outside those times there are fewer distractions. The plus side is that there are always people to chat to or to have lunch with, and there is a good social side to my job.

4

Deciding Whether to Become a Barrister

Before embarking on a demanding, expensive, and, for some, frankly depressing path to becoming a barrister, you should take an afternoon to really think about whether you're cut out for life at the Bar. It is not a question of bravado and confidence, it is a question of what you like and what you are good at. One of the main aims of this book is to familiarise you with the world of the Bar so you can know whether you will fit into it, but I would strongly advise that you read the novels and watch the television series listed at the end of this book in order to really get a feel for the Bar (as well as doing **mini-pupillages** if you can), so as to decide whether you like it or hate it. The idea of standing on your feet, sometimes under-prepared and on the losing side, arguing in a court in front of 20 people in a wig and gown against some pompous ass with an **Oxbridge** accent is not everyone's idea of a good time (whether or not you are a just as pompous and have the same accent).

The important question is really whether you want to be a barrister more than you want to do any other job, but in practice it often comes down to a decision between being a barrister and a solicitor, and so a comparison between the two (as follows) is a useful way of teasing out some of the features of the Bar. Don't forget, however, that there are a huge range of non-law jobs out there (as well as a few other legal jobs such as patent agent, **legal executive**, legal secretary, etc) and you should think carefully about them. Even if you have a law degree you don't have to become a lawyer. It is worth remembering that most people other than lawyers do not do a job related to their degree.

Barristers are often perceived as being grander, more old-fashioned, and more arrogant than solicitors: this comes from the wigs and robes, the old buildings, **the Inns**, and the traditions. This may be because, in **litigation** involving barristers, the barrister sits in front and addresses the court while the solicitors sit behind (although that does not mean that it is not the solicitors who are running the litigation strategy, and also we should not forget that most lower court advocacy is conducted by solicitors). I must confess that I never really doubted my desire to be a barrister, but for a time the one thing putting me off (when I was aged about 17) was that all barristers seemed to me to be arrogant and objectionable. It turned out that either I was wrong or I became like that, because I do not find this nowadays, but certainly the old-fashioned features of the Bar are little more than window-dressing to most of what a barrister does. However, that does not mean that barristers are the same as solicitors. The famous American judge Oliver Wendell Holmes once said that the reason for England's split profession (ie the division of lawyers into solicitors and barristers) had been explained to him by a barrister as follows: '*if law was to be practised, somebody had to be damned, and he preferred that it should be somebody else*'.[21] This is probably unfair and inaccurate, but it gives the flavour of the way many barristers feel.

If you are sensible, you are probably going to decide whether to be a barrister or a solicitor on the basis of the following four factors: 1) what you want to spend your time actually doing during the many working hours of the day; 2) whether you want to be employed or self-employed; 3) whether you have the grades and skills; and 4) whether you can afford it.

WHAT YOU WANT TO SPEND YOUR TIME DOING

The most important consideration should also be the most obvious, and yet this is the consideration that most people overlook. When choosing whether to be a barrister or solicitor (or whether to do any job for that matter), you have to consider what you are going to spend 40 or 50 of the 80 waking hours from Monday to Friday actually doing. As you will already have realised, what you do as a barrister will depend upon what area of law you work in and what type of chambers or other organisation you are in. Similarly, what you do as

---

[21] 'Law in Science and Science in Law' (1899) 7 *Harvard Law Review* 443, at 460.

a solicitor will depend upon what type of solicitors' firm or other employer you are working for. You must get experience of both (and so you should definitely do a vacation placement at a solicitors' firm even if you are pretty sure you want to be a barrister). However, it is still fair to say that if you prefer spending hour after hour doing the things on one of the following lists then you will probably prefer the job that goes with it:

Barrister's activities	Solicitor's activities
• researching a point of law in the library and online; • writing a legal opinion on a point of law; • reading files of evidence (letters, transcripts of interviews, etc); • speaking, and handling witnesses, in court; • drafting claims and other court documents; • sitting on the train; • sitting in conferences; • managing paper and emails • managing paper and emails	• liaising with people (the **lay client**, the witnesses, etc); • working out what the client's problem is and how it might be solved; • reading files of evidence (letters, transcripts of interviews, etc); • perhaps speaking, and handling witnesses, in court; • managing people; • writing letters outmanoeuvring the other side; • sitting in conferences;

EMPLOYED OR SELF-EMPLOYED

The next question is whether you want to be employed or self-employed. As you will have learned, a certain proportion of barristers are employed, and some solicitors work in firms so small that they are basically self-employed, but generally speaking, barristers are self-employed and solicitors are employed. This is not a mere technicality, as quite a lot follows from this, and some people are much better suited to one or the other (although, of course, some people will thrive in either environment):

Being self-employed in chambers	Being employed in a fairly big law firm
Flexi-time: you can go home and take holidays when you want to. Although you often have to work late or at the week end to meet a deadline, you can choose whether you work in the morning or the evening or on Saturday or Sunday. However, you are not paid a wage so holidays are doubly expensive: you are not only paying for the holiday, you are also not earning.	Hours and holiday entitlement set by your employer, although you may still have to work late or at the weekend to meet a deadline. Paid holidays.
Organise your own workload: you choose how much work to take on and you are responsible for doing it. As a barrister it is rarely possible to pass work off to others.	*Work is shared:* work is often allocated to you (at least when you are junior), although often as part of a team so that it can be shared out if it gets too much.
Organise your own finances: you (with the help of your clerks and probably an accountant) must be organised and keep money aside to pay your taxes, your pension, and your chambers expenses, and must make sufficient provision for work expenses such as travel, computer equipment, etc.	*Waged:* you get paid a wage so all the tax is calculated and deducted for you, your pension may be taken out of your wage, and your employer provides your equipment.
Work alone: you generally work alone on your task and you alone are responsible for it (with no one to check it), although you will often have meetings with solicitors and will sometimes be led by a **silk**. The buck stops with you: if you screw up, you will be sued personally (although you will have insurance).	*Teamwork:* you often work within a team of two or more solicitors, or at least under supervision, although some solicitors handle most of their cases alone. If you screw up, your firm and not you will get sued, although, of course, they won't be pleased.
Paid by the hour: a fair amount of the time you will be paid by the hour so if it takes all night, at least you are getting paid for it. The financial incentive makes you a good service-provider.	*Paid a wage:* unless you are paid for overtime, generally you have to do as many hours as it takes without any (extra) financial reward or incentive.

No surrounding company: you can socialise, but ultimately you're a one-man or one-woman business and there is no central organiser laying on events or facilities. Many barristers do little socialising with their work colleagues.	*Part of a company:* you may be part of a big company with a gym, football team, bonding days out, and a cafeteria.
No benefits, only cash: if you want a pension and health insurance you have to pay for it yourself.	*Benefits:* your employer will have a pension plan, and probably health cover, and occasional tickets in a box at the new Emirates Stadium to watch Arsenal.
Relaxed dress code: barristers in many chambers will dress down whenever they are not expecting to be in court or to see clients (although with a suit on the back of the door just in case).	You wear a suit, every day.
The chambers environment: you will probably have your own room, or share with one other. The decor is likely to be old-fashioned, and (especially in London) your building will be in a nice green area.	*The firm environment:* you may well share your room or work in an open-plan office, probably with modern facilities but often in a grey area of the city.

WHETHER YOU HAVE THE GRADES FROM A GOOD UNIVERSITY AND THE QUALITIES REQUIRED

It is important to be realistic. Unless you have (or will get) an upper second or a first-class honours degree from a good university,[22] you probably won't get your foot in the door of any chambers that you are interested in. Often, although not always, it is that simple. If you have a lower second, or an upper second from a weaker university, it is still possible, but you may need superb contacts or non-academic experience, or alternatively need to be very flexible and persevering and to consider indirect routes to the Bar (such as through first becoming a solicitor). Some areas of the Bar (eg commercial and **Chancery** work) have stricter academic requirements than others (eg criminal and

[22] By good university I mean one in the top 10 or 15 of *The Times* or the *Guardian* university league tables for law.

general common law). This does not mean that you will walk into a job as a solicitor if you have a lower second-class degree, but your chances are higher than if you try for the Bar.

As far as skills/qualities are concerned, the ancient Greeks used to consult an oracle in Delphi upon which was inscribed '*Gnothi sauton*', which means 'know thyself'. I'm surprised anyone ever had to ask the oracle a question, because the advice 'know thyself' will solve most problems one can encounter. You will frequently mislead others about your strengths or weaknesses, but try not to lie to yourself. Ask yourself whether you have most of the following qualities. I suppose you could do a psychometric test, but deep down you know if your written English is rubbish or you are shy or are not that honest. Although different types of barrister use the following qualities to varying extents, if you do not have them, you probably shouldn't be a barrister:

Qualities needed for the Bar (in approximately decreasing order of importance):

- *intellect:* you must be intelligent and so potentially able to solve arcane and abstract questions either on reflection or on the spot, rather than merely clever and able to solve practical problems (although being clever is also useful). A good barrister is good at analysis, which means taking a complex real-life case and working out which legal principles apply and which facts/pieces of evidence are relevant to particular arguments;
- *diligence and application:* in other words, you must be a hard worker. Success both in and out of court is usually largely a result of time-consuming, often boring, preparation and graft. If you are not willing to put in the hours, often late at night, then the Bar is not for you;
- *integrity:* you must be an ethical person and must not be afraid of sticking to the rules of your profession and your honour, and keeping the confidences of your client. It sounds cheesy, but it comes up in one form or another just about every week of a barrister's life;
- *advocacy skills:* the art of persuasion involves forcefully and clearly articulating your arguments in their best light, and as well as oral communication skills (being a good speaker, preferably quick on your feet and witty), it also requires good judgement and intellect in order to persuasively choose what to say and when to say it;

- *written communication skills:* similar skills to those of advocacy, although being a quick thinker is less important here and being good with grammar and English generally is more important;
- *organisational ability:* you must be able to organise yourself and your work because there will be no one else to do it for you. If you are disorganised you will screw things up, run out of money, and lose clients;
- *confidence:* you must be confident of your own ability, often bordering on arrogant, but confidence will come in time and is not as important as many of the other characteristics;
- *discretion:* you will learn a lot of confidential things from clients and must be careful not to release confidential details when discussing your cases with other barristers or with friends and family;
- *general interpersonal skills:* being chatty, remembering names, and being able to command a meeting are all very useful abilities;
- *numeracy:* being good with figures is helpful, and is essential for commercial and tax barristers;
- *IT:* you will probably have to be pretty good with computers (but then who doesn't these days?).

WHETHER YOU CAN AFFORD IT

Sad but true: despite the increasing pupillage awards and the generous scholarships from the Inns, unless you are the cream of the cream (and so likely to receive the maximum scholarship funding) or have wealthy parents, going to the Bar means getting into (or at least risking getting into) a lot of debt with no immediate way out. This results from unpaid work experience, an expensive vocational course, and a year of often underpaid pupillage—and that's if everything goes well! In contrast, medium-sized and larger solicitors' firms would fund your **Legal Practice Course** fees, pay a decent wage during your **training contract**, and ultimately your chances of getting a job as an associate solicitor after a training contract are higher than the chances of tenancy following pupillage.

Taking into account living expenses, going to the Bar after university will cost at least a further £20,000 (ie in addition to debts accrued during your undergraduate degree) if you did a law degree, and more if you have to do the **CPE/GDL** year as well, and it is highly unlikely that you will get all of this paid for by scholarships and fairly likely that none of it will be paid for. Of course, it's not all doom and gloom: if you do get tenancy then, depending upon the area of practice, you will probably pay off your debts fairly quickly (as the banks, who are willing to lend to prospective barristers, well know). Even if you don't become a barrister there are quite a lot of other fairly well-paid jobs available to the unemployed barrister (including as a solicitor).

5

An Overview of Qualification

SOME CHILLING STATISTICS

On the evidence of recent years, in any one year, approximately:
2,900 students apply to the BVC,
1,700 get a BVC place,
1,250 pass the BVC,
560 get pupillage,
500 get tenancy (estimated).

Thus, under one in five of those who apply to the BVC, and under one in three of those who cough up the £10,000 or so for the BVC, make it to practising as a self-employed barrister.

To become a barrister a person must complete the following key steps (see also the timetables at the end of this book and the one at http://www.chambersandpartners.com/chambersstudent).

1) THE SCHOOL STAGE

School preparation for a career as a barrister is not really within the scope of this book. For further information, readers should see Barnard, O'Sullivan, and Virgo, *What About Law?* (Oxford, Hart Publishing, 2007). I confine myself, therefore, to the following observations: the most important thing is to get high A level grades. The actual subjects are not important (sciences are fine, although arts/humanities/languages are more likely to develop your written and oral communication skills), save that it is probably best not to do A level law if you are going to go on to do a law degree because it may be more likely to teach you bad habits and to give you half-baked ideas than to put you at an advantage. Taking GCSE law, however, is sensible if you want to find out a bit more about law (although I personally think it is not necessary and you may well be better off studying something else at that stage). Also, if you can get involved in the Bar National Mock Trial Competition, which is open to all secondary schools and further education colleges, it is well worth doing so.[23]

2) THE LAW DEGREE/LAW CONVERSION COURSE STAGE

Unless you transfer from another legal profession or jurisdiction (see chapter fourteen), in order to become a barrister you must go down one of the following three routes. Before discussing the three routes, a few general points should be made about this university stage of the qualification to the Bar:

> Of those who obtain a pupillage, around 25 per cent got a first-class degree, around 60 per cent got an upper second, and around 15 per cent got a lower second.

Whether you do a law degree, or a non-law degree and then a law conversion course (as discussed below), the most important thing is that you get a good degree. You need a lower second to get a place on the BVC, but without an upper second many chambers won't look at you at all (and even the BVC may soon raise its minimum requirements above a lower second). The importance of this should not be underestimated, but nor should it be overstated: a first is neither necessary nor sufficient; I know of stellar candidates with top firsts who could not get pupillage, and those with lower seconds who could, although both groups are outside the norm. If you are currently a student, and

[23] See http://www.citizenshipfoundation.org.uk/main/comps.php?21.

want to be a barrister, then I advise you to take serious steps towards making sure of an upper second (ie knuckling down and cutting down your social life) before it is too late.

A word should be said about Oxford and Cambridge. The Bar, particularly the London Bar, has more than its fair share of **Oxbridge** law and non-law graduates (between a quarter and a third of new entrants). This does not mean that people from other universities are frowned upon, it just means that there is quite a lot of discussion about the Oxford or Cambridge colleges people studied at, who lectured them, and such things. Such discussions can make non-Oxford and Cambridge people feel excluded, but in my experience it goes no further than that: there is no bar to graduates of other universities doing well, and no preference for Oxford and Cambridge people over graduates of the other equally strong law departments.

While at university you will probably not get much career support. Even if you are in a law department, and so are likely to go on to be a barrister or solicitor, you will be treated (with some justification) as if you are studying history or similar and left to find out about careers yourself. It is you, and not your university, that should be most interested in your career, so there are no excuses for not doing the two key things (apart from getting a good degree) to help your chances: mooting and mini-pupillages. Mini-pupillages are discussed below in chapter six, but it's worth taking a moment briefly to introduce mooting here: **Mooting** is the argument of pretend cases in front of pretend (or sometimes real) judges. Moots are often simulations of appeals (a hearing in a higher court of argument that the lower court decided the case wrongly), and so do not often involve witnesses and generally turn on points of law (just like real appeals). Mooters generally moot in teams of two. I cannot emphasise enough how important it is to do as much mooting as you can. If your university law department or college or student law society does not organise its own mooting competitions, then you can either organise one yourself (it is not that hard and there is usually at least one cooperative law lecturer who used to be a barrister) or get yourself entered on behalf of the university into the inter-university, or even international, competitions. If your university does not have a history of entering then you may be able to represent your university at mooting without having to compete against anyone to do so. Unlike with most things, it is true in this case that taking part is more important than winning, and there can be no excuse for getting to a pupillage interview without having done a moot (although many people do). Start at www.mootingnet.org.uk, which has details of the inter-university mooting competitions and explains where to begin (helpfully starting with the immortal phrase 'Don't Panic'). There are a couple of mooting books that are also worth splashing out on, notable John Snape and Gary Watt's *The Cavendish Guide to Mooting* (London, Routledge Cavendish, 2006) and Dan Hill and David Pope's *Sweet & Maxwell Guide to Mooting* (London, Sweet & Maxwell, 2006).

I will now set out the three routes through university to a career at the Bar. It should be remembered that after all three of the routes,[24] it is still necessary to go on to do a BVC and all the other stages (4 and following) listed below.

i) A Law Degree

A qualifying law degree (not my term) basically means any degree that satisfies the Bar Standards Board's definition of law degree. Just about every three- or four-year law degree in England and Wales satisfies this definition, including most joint honours courses: in a nutshell it has to cover contract law, tort law (the law of wrongs), criminal law, the law of equity and trusts, the law of the European Union, land law, and **public law** (constitutional and administrative law).[25] If your degree is not a qualifying law degree, but did include at least four law courses (eg as a 'minor'), then you will still have to do the CPE or GDL (see the next section) but should be able to get an exemption from having to repeat the particular law courses you've already done (although if you have done three or fewer law courses in your undergraduate degree you'll still have to do the whole CPE or GDL, repeating those courses).

ii) A Non-law Degree and then a One-year Law Degree

The main alternative to doing a qualifying law degree is to do a non-law degree and then a one-year **CPE** (Common Professional Examination) or **GDL** (Graduate Diploma in Law). To do the CPE/GDL, you must have at least a lower second-class non-law degree. All full-time CPE/GDL courses must be applied for, usually

---

[24] Save in the case of the **exempting law degree** at the University of Northumbria.

[25] There is also a special type of qualifying law degree, currently offered only by the University of Northumbria, which is known as an '**exempting law degree**' because it integrates both a qualifying law degree and the Bar Vocational Course into one course.

online, through www.lawcabs.ac.uk, with applications for part-time courses being made directly to the relevant institution. The main closing date for applications is the start of the February before the course is due to commence. The application form is of the usual type, focusing on education and legal experience, with the main time-consuming part being a box for up to 1,500 characters on '*Further personal information, eg relevant experience, reasons for choosing law, career aspirations, hobbies, interests, etc*'. The CPE/GDL is hard work, fitting into a year what takes about two years in the undergraduate law degree (ie all the core courses but not any optional ones), but by the time you get round to it you should be more focused and experienced than during your first undergraduate degree. These days around 25 per cent of barristers have been down this route, and they are not at a disadvantage as against those who did an undergraduate law degree (save that they know a bit less law), and indeed in one or two technical areas of law (and patent work springs to mind), only science (and not straight law) graduates will be eligible because of the real or perceived need to be comfortable in the scientific world in which the cases arise.

Even though the CPE/GDL is taken before the **BVC** or **LPC** and is taken by potential solicitors as well as potential barristers, in many of the institutions providing these courses the students who express an interest in the Bar are grouped together in classes of would-be barristers, which is handy for making contacts and sharing tips.

As with BVC students, the **Inns** provide significant scholarships to CPE/GDL students (up to £10,000 per person). The deadline for applications is the April before the course starts, and the procedure is similar to that described below for the BVC (and note that there is nothing to stop you applying to your Inn for scholarships at every stage for which scholarships are offered: CPE/GDL, BVC, and pupillage).

One further point that may be of interest is that, as from 2006, anyone who does both a GDL and then the BVC (or LPC) at the College of Law (one of the many places where you can do these courses) will be automatically awarded an **LLB** honours undergraduate law degree. In other words, in addition to their non-law undergraduate degree and their vocational qualifications, they will also have an undergraduate law degree, which is likely to make the GDL route more attractive than it would otherwise be. The class of the degree will depend on adding how well you did on the GDL to how well you did on the BVC. Doubtless the other institutions that teach these courses will lobby for the same powers, but at the time of writing the College of Law is unique in this respect.

iii)   A Non-law Degree and then a Two-year Law Degree

There is a lesser-known middle way, often called a '**senior status law degree**', taken, like the CPE/GDL, after a non-law degree. This is a two year qualifying law degree which is fuller than the CPE/GDL (for example, it often includes a dissertation or optional advanced courses in addition to the basic compulsory courses) but shorter than an undergraduate law course. It is offered by some of the strong universities that do not teach the CPE/GDL, such as Oxford, Cambridge, and Leeds, and at some of the institutions, the resulting degree is labelled a 'Master's' (which is handy in terms of letters after your name). A list of the institutions providing these courses is available at http://www.lawsociety.org.uk/documents/downloads/becomingdegreessnr.pdf. I'm surprised these degrees are not more popular, because in many ways they are the best of both worlds since, while the CPE/GDL is generally a high-quality intensive course, it can still lead to a steep learning curve upon commencement of **pupillage** at the Bar, where legal understanding is paramount, as well as requiring its students to do **mini-pupillages** and pupillage interviews when they have done less than a year of law. I understand that places on senior status law degree courses are limited and competition for them is fairly fierce.

3)   OTHER STAGES: JOBS, FURTHER DEGREES, ETC

Not everyone goes straight from school to university, or from university to doing the Bar Vocational Course. The fastest student who had no 'time out' would be on the BVC at 21 or 22 (depending upon whether he or she took the law degree or the non-law degree routes). However, about a third of those on the BVC are over 26, so the reader can see that it is far from unusual to come from another career. Many people only realise or decide that they want to be barristers after having already pursued other careers for five, 10, or more years. Whether these careers are related to spheres in which barristers work (eg accountancy, fund management, the police, and the media) or not, this sort of experience is welcome: experience of the world and of working with people (and the maturity and gravitas it brings) can only help.

Even if you know that you want to go to the Bar, you may want to do other things first. To be honest, I did not feel sufficiently mature at 21 to go to the Bar and, therefore, to have my own clients at 23 (in the **second six** months of my pupillage), so I did a master's law degree (an **LLM**) and worked as a lecturer for three years. Other alternatives for a short break are to work for a year as a research assistant at the Law Commission, as a paralegal at a solicitors' firm or as a court clerk. These can all help your chances of pupillage (and earn you money to pay for the BVC). See further the jobs and work experience set out in chapter six. However, it should be noted that it is still usual to go straight through from university, so you shouldn't feel obliged to take time out in between if you don't want to.

4) JOINING AN INN

Before you can do the BVC, you must join an **Inn of Court**. What they are, how to choose between them, and how and when to apply, are all described further in chapter seven. For now, it is only necessary to clarify what an Inn is not. As explained in chapter one, although some chambers are physically located in the Inns of Court grounds, it is a **chambers** and not an Inn of Court that gives you **pupillage** and **tenancy**. Further, you cannot do the **BVC** at an Inn of Court, rather you do it at a **Bar school**: although one of the Bar schools is called the 'Inns of Court School of Law', this is not an Inn of Court and is just one of the several Bar schools at which you can do the BVC.

Soon after joining an Inn you will probably also want to apply to the Inn for a scholarship to help fund your BVC; this is discussed in chapter eight.

5) APPLYING FOR AND GETTING PUPILLAGE

There is no fixed time at which a would-be barrister must obtain a pupillage place. Many students are awarded a pupillage one and a bit, or even two and a bit, years before their pupillages begin. This has the significant advantage that the student goes into the BVC (with its concomitant expense) knowing that he or she will have a pupillage at the end of it. However, a significant proportion (perhaps half) of the students on the BVC don't have a pupillage lined up when they do the BVC, and these students make pupillage applications during the BVC year. Many finish the BVC with no pupillage place to go to, and it can take a year or more after that before they get pupillage, if they ever do. How to get a pupillage is discussed below (see especially chapter ten).

6) THE BAR VOCATIONAL COURSE (BVC) STAGE

The next stage is the **BVC**. This is a one-year full-time or two-year part-time course, and you need to commence the BVC within six years of completing the academic stage, that is, within six years of your law degree or conversion course. The BVC is discussed further in chapter eight.

7) THE REQUIREMENTS OF THE INN AND THE CALL TO THE BAR

Student members of each **Inn** must complete the necessary **dining** and other **qualifying sessions**, and ultimately get **called** to the Bar by their Inn. These requirements are explained below in chapter nine.

8) THE PUPILLAGE

Pupillage is the barrister's apprenticeship, although some people see it as a year-long interview. The year of pupillage can be 'magnificently out of the ordinary' (Charlotte Buckhaven, *Barrister By and Large* (London, Pan Books 1985), p 13), but it can also be traumatic. You will need to commence pupillage within five years of completing your BVC, and during pupillage you must complete certain compulsory courses provided by your **Inn** and others. See further below in chapters ten to twelve.

9) GETTING TAKEN ON (TENANCY)

The final step is successfully to be invited to become a **tenant** of your chambers when your pupillage has been completed. If you are not invited to become a tenant, you must try to find another chambers. Some chambers will **take on** tenants who have not done pupillage there, but many will require you to do a **third six** pupillage, in other words to do six more months of practising pupillage before they decide whether to offer you tenancy. Not many chambers offer third sixes, and it is not done on such an open marketplace as that for first and second sixes. It is really a question of looking at the notice boards in the Inns of Court and getting people in your chambers to contact people they know in other chambers.

If you can't find somewhere to do a third six, some chambers will allow you to stay on in chambers without becoming a tenant: this is called 'squatting'. As a squatter you are not a pupil so you must have your own **professional indemnity insurance**. Essentially, you will be practising on your own account from within a chambers, but on a temporary basis.

Of course, some people who don't get tenancy leave the Bar and go to solicitors' firms or other jobs.

TO SAVE MONEY LATER, START KEEPING RECEIPTS NOW

If you become a self-employed barrister, you will then pay income tax. When calculating your taxable revenue (ie income) as a barrister for the purposes of working out how much income tax to pay, the Inland Revenue permits you to deduct business-related expenditure (which must be wholly and exclusively for business use) that you personally (ie not your parents) have incurred for the *seven years prior to your commencing practice as a self-employed barrister*. Exactly what is included is a matter for your accountant, but the best thing is to keep receipts from everything that might be covered, including Bar school (BVC) fees, wig and gown, computers and related equipment, stationery, law books, and possibly costs incurred during a law undergraduate degree/GDL or CPE/master's law degree. Quite apart from income tax, you may also be able later to get the VAT back on items bought in the three years prior to your registering for VAT, which you will probably do upon commencement of practice after pupillage. The upshot of this is that if you pay £500 including VAT for a wig and gown, and the like, keeping the receipt will save you around £160 (consisting of £75 VAT back and around £95 saving on your income tax bill). Think what you can save on £13,000 of Bar school fees . . .

6

Work Experience: Mini-pupillages and Other Legal Experience

WHAT ARE MINI-PUPILLAGES?

A **mini-pupillage**, shortened to 'mini', is nothing more than work experience at a chambers. It usually lasts for between a day and a week (three days is perhaps optimal) and is unpaid in all but a very few chambers. The name 'mini-pupillage' suggests, quite rightly, that the mini-pupillage is like a very short **pupillage**. The **mini-pupil** (ie you) will usually sit in the barrister's room reading the papers in one of the barrister's cases, or follow the barrister to court or to meetings, much as a pupil would do. The mini-pupil will often be put with different barristers, for perhaps a day or half a day with each, in order to meet a variety of people.

In most (although not all) mini-pupillages, the mini-pupil supervisors (ie the barristers who look after the mini-pupil) will fill out a form or orally pass on their views of the mini-pupils to some central committee, which information may be looked at if the mini-pupil applies for pupillage. However, some mini-pupillages are actually described as **assessed mini-pupillages**, which means that the mini-pupils are on notice that the mini-pupillage is part of the pupillage application process and they will be scrutinised. In many mini-pupillages the mini-pupil will be asked to do a piece of written work, but in an assessed mini-pupillage this work will be more important, and more formally assessed, than in an unassessed mini-pupillage.

WHAT TO GET OUT OF THEM

A mini-pupillage is one of the few ways of finding out what it is like to be a barrister, and a barrister at that chambers in particular. Keep your eyes open and ask questions. (However, although you should not be too scared to ask, it is unfortunately not true that there is no such thing as a stupid question.) If you get to talk to the junior tenants or current pupils all the better: you will be able to tell if they are stressed, and whether they are treated well and genuinely like their chambers. Also, just as useful as information about the chambers you are at is the information you get about other chambers. It is only by gathering and collating the snippets of information about other chambers (*this* chambers didn't take anyone on this year, *that* chambers is only interested in how much money it makes, *this* chambers can be sexist, *that* chambers is very friendly . . .) that you can get a feel for what the different chambers are like. When you get home in the evening, take a note of who you met and who supervised you and what cases you saw. You will forget otherwise, and this information can be useful when you come to have pupillage interviews months or years later.

Remember that you are on show and that the people you are sitting with are self-employed, and are often the junior members of the chambers and so the least relaxed about their work and where their next meal is coming from. Although this only goes so far, to an extent you should treat them as if they are doing you a favour. Of course, there are good and bad ways of making your mark. In the height of summer, I did a mini-pupillage with a very good and very friendly commercial set. Before a hearing I was standing waiting in the corridors of the Commercial Court in the St Dunstan's House building on New Fetter Lane (a building near the **RCJ** that is soon to be completely rebuilt) with my mini-pupil supervisor. The corridor was packed with about 40 people waiting to go into court, although most of them weren't involved with our case (thank goodness). The corridor was most certainly not air-conditioned. After about an hour we got in to court, and I sat on the very back row with two students doing vacation placements while the barristers and **instructing solicitors** sat in the main seats doing their stuff. About 20 minutes in, my skin felt cold and clammy, and an instant later I found myself lying on the floor. I had fainted, although was only unconscious for a second. The judge asked if I was okay and the court clerk took me outside and plied me with water. Everyone was very sympathetic, saying that the building was terribly stuffy, etc, although I felt that I had aggravated matters by being dehydrated after a few drinks the night before. Anyway, a year or two later they offered me a pupillage through **OLPAS**, so I don't know what moral can be drawn from that story. In a cowardly manner, I later told that story to the barrister I was against in my first hearing in the Commercial Court, saying that the whole thing had happened to a mini-pupil at our chambers. Probably he guessed.

After the mini is over you may well want to send a thank-you email or, even better, a note to the particular barristers who looked after you. I don't think I sent any when I did mini-pupillages, but I've since received a few, and it does give a good impression, as well as being the polite thing to do.

WHERE AND WHEN TO DO YOUR MINIS

Where you do your minis depends upon the stage you are at, both in terms of your education and training and in terms of your decision-making. First, perhaps while at school, it is worth trying to do a mini-pupillage at any chambers you can get one at (perhaps near to where you live), to get a feel for what a barrister does. If you are still at school most chambers won't give you a mini, so if your family or friends have contacts with a barrister, now might be the time to use them. Don't worry if you can't get any minis at this stage. Then, perhaps in your first year of legal study at university (ie during your law degree or CPE/GDL), try to do mini-pupillages at a range of chambers to enable you to make the key decisions (London or non-London; criminal or civil; within civil, Chancery or commercial or mixed common law; etc). Once you've honed in on an area and are preparing to apply for pupillages in the next year or two, you will want to do minis at as many of the chambers to which you may want to apply as possible. Finally, if you find you have applied for pupillage, or have even been offered one, and still haven't done a mini-pupillage at the relevant chambers, then you really must do one before you sign up for a possible 40 years at the place. Mini-pupillages feature in the timetables set out later on in this book, although they can in truth be done at any time (subject to each chambers' policy). For those doing the CPE/GDL, there is obviously much less time in which to do minis, so you may have to be more focused about it (and give up all your holidays to minis).

HOW TO GET MINIS

Solicitors' firms provide 'vacation placements', which are often paid and crowned by a drinks party. The downside of these is that they usually require completion of a long application form with questions such as 'describe a situation in which you worked within a team to solve a problem'. Fortunately (and unlike solicitors' firms) most chambers require only a CV and covering letter, and not many chambers interview applicants for mini-pupillages. Check the chambers website and research the details, checking whether the mini-pupillage is funded or (more likely) unfunded, and whether it is **assessed** or not. Read all about the chambers (just as you will when preparing to apply for pupillage, as discussed below).

As mentioned, if you are still at school or very early in your first degree then you may find it difficult to get a mini-pupillage unless you or your family know somebody at the chambers. If you are in your second or final year of a law degree or are about to start your CPE then most chambers will accept you if you look like the sort of candidate who might get a pupillage later on in the process. In other words, only apply if you think you and the chambers may suit each other (although it will be too early for either of you to be sure).

Barristers are good communicators, careful about what they draft, and not flashy. Your CV and covering letter should reflect this: make no typographical, grammatical, or other errors. Do not use flashy fonts and colours. Be clear and neat. There are myriad books about how to write CVs out there, so I will confine myself to the following further tips:

(i)   keep it to two pages at most;
(ii)   when setting things out in chronological order (eg education, employment experience) start with the most recent and finish with the least recent;
(iii) make the level of detail proportionate to the relevance (both in terms of content and how long ago something was): do mention non-legal experience and hobbies, but don't relate the minutiae of how you put in place a new stock-control system at the charity shop you worked in;
(iv)   cut to the chase: the reader should be able quickly to see your personal details, educational experience (including grades and prizes), work history and work experience, and any mooting or debating experience, which are the things he or she really cares about, so put these things (under suitable headings and probably

in the order listed above) before information about the silver-service waitering, hockey team, and burgeoning interest in the philosophy of William James (all of which have been on my own CV at one time or another);

(v) barristers are unlikely to be impressed with an introductory paragraph setting out your skills, career plans and why you think you will be a great barrister (although this may be quite suitable in CVs for other jobs) so save this material, where relevant, for the covering letter.

The covering letter should tell the reader what stage you are at (in terms of education and career progress), should perhaps give a couple of *relevant* highlights of your achievements, should mention something about why you want to do a mini at the particular chambers (be honest and understated: 'to confirm my anticipated interest in tax law' is better than 'because your chambers is the best and I want to work with the best' or other such drivel), and suggest a few weeks in which you are available to do the mini-pupillage at dates to suit the chambers. The most common mistake in the covering letter, fatal to any application for mini-pupillages (or pupillages), is to use a standard form letter (which is understandable) but to fail to change all the parts of the letter that need changing (which is unforgivable). As you might expect, if a particular criminal chambers gets a letter that includes a paragraph praising one of its competitors, or referring to its reputation for family law (which this chambers does not do), then that letter goes straight in the bin, at least once a critical note has been put next to the name of the applicant.

OTHER LEGAL EXPERIENCE (PAID AND UNPAID)

There are a variety of jobs and other activities that you might do before or after, or in some cases during, your **BVC,** that can dramatically improve your CV and barristerial skills. One of the key things you will have to demonstrate on your CV, and, later, on your **OLPAS** form, is your commitment to the law and legal practice. The following are those that spring to mind, although what stage you do them, whether they pay, and how much time they take up, depends upon the particularly opportunity.

- *Research assistant at the Law Commission.* The Law Commission sometimes recruits one or two research assistants for a year, working full time. These are prestigious posts and are advertised at http://www.lawcom.gov.uk/ working.htm.
- *Outdoor clerk.* Often solicitors instruct barristers to attend civil hearings and don't bother to attend themselves. Sometimes, however, they want a full note of what went on and may employ an outdoor clerk to go to court and sit behind the barrister and take notes. The pay is not too bad (usually from £45 to £60 for the day) and can give you good contacts and experience. Contact the big solicitors' firms directly, or see http://www.lpc-law.co.uk.
- *Paralegal.* A paralegal is someone who is not qualified as a barrister, solicitor, or legal executive, but often has a law degree, and provides legal and administrative support services to solicitors. The pay is pretty good, and you'll get at least some relevant experience. Go to the legal recruitment agencies.
- *Clerk, or 'legal adviser', in a magistrates' court.* This is a full-time job, advertised in January or February, working as an assistant and adviser on points of law and practice to magistrates, who are not legally trained. You sit in the court and watch the case, and assist when necessary. You must have done the BVC but often do not need to have done your pupillage, so this is a good thing to do after your BVC while you are applying for pupillages or waiting for pupillage to start, particularly if you are interested in the criminal Bar. See further http://www.hmcourts-service.gov.uk/vacancies.htm.
- *Judicial assistant in the Court of Appeal.* Modelled on the US judicial clerking system, this is a full-time job for three to 12 (but usually at least six) months as an assistant to one or more of the judges in the Court of Appeal. Among other things, the assistants summarise cases for the judges and assist them with research and drafting speeches. These positions are very competitive (there are ten per year) and are advertised three times per year (for the three court terms). There is not a fixed point in a career at which to do these assistant-ships, although it is probably more common to do so after pupillage than before pupillage. See further http://www.hmcourts-service.gov.uk/cms/7629.htm.
- *Working at the **Free Representation Unit** (**FRU**) (unpaid).* This enables you to represent real clients in real cases at **tribunals** where no rights of audience are needed to appear (eg employment and social security tribunals). This is excellent experience and great for the CV, although I understand that many people don't get past the

fairly exacting practice cases you have to do to qualify as an FRU worker (not because it's too hard, but because they are too disorganised) and so never do any work for the real clients. This is a waste of their time as far as their CV is concerned because when they are asked about FRU at their interviews, they will be asked about what real cases they have done. FRU is most useful for those hoping to go into social security and employment tribunals, but the experience is good for all prospective barristers. See further http://www.freerepresentationunit.org.uk/. (The equivalent for qualified barristers is the **Bar Pro Bono Unit**.)

• *Other legal or related volunteer work (unpaid)*. Students with some time to spare can volunteer at legal clinics, law centres and Citizens Advice Bureaux around the country. Most **Bar schools** have some sort of **pro bono** clinic or advice centre and are increasingly encouraging their students to get involved, although students shouldn't forget about the majority of such centres which are completely independent of the Bar schools. The amount of commitment and the length of the training varies, but these are good ways to get practical experience (often in an area of law you may end up practising in) and to show that you generally are interested in helping people with legal problems. See further http://www.lawcentres.org.uk; http://www.citizensadvice.org.uk. Another option is to volunteer at your local court's victim or witness support service, providing support and guidance to victims or witnesses: see http://www. victimsupport.org.uk/vs_england_wales.

• *Other*. There are various other jobs out there, including administrative jobs in legal organisations and legal research jobs. See notice boards in your Inn or Bar school and those of the legal recruitment agencies, including those online such as http://www.lawcareers.net, http://www.totallylegal.com/, and http://www.legalprospects.co.uk.

7

Joining an Inn

MORE ABOUT THE INNS

As indicated earlier, barristers used to learn their trade in **the Inns**, living a university-type life of lectures by **Benchers**, of **mooting** and debating, and of learning formal court documents by heart. Nowadays the Inns serve fewer purposes, one of them being to make Law London really beautiful—Nathaniel Hawthorne's description of the Inns (he's talking specifically of **Gray's Inn**) is as true today as when he wrote it:

> It is very strange to find so much of ancient quietude right in the monster city's very jaws, which yet the monster shall not eat up,—right in its very belly, indeed, which yet, in all these ages, it shall not digest and convert into the same substance as the rest of its bustling streets. Nothing else in London is so like the effect of a spell, as to pass under one of these archways, and find yourself transported from the jumble, mob, tumult, uproar, as of an age of weekdays condensed into the present hour, into what seems an eternal Sabbath.
>
> (6 December 1867 entry, *Passages from the English Notebooks of Nathaniel Hawthorne* (Boston, Fields, Osgood, 1870))

The four Inns (Gray's, Inner Temple, Lincoln's and Middle Temple) are open to the public during daylight hours, and their gardens are open over lunchtime periods, so anyone can (and should) have a wander around. Apart from the Inn facilities (library, impressive dining halls, quadrangles, and gardens), the Inns are principally made up of tall stair-welled buildings. These are usually leased by chambers, although the top floors are reserved for flats that are rented as pieds-a-terre for judges and other legal luminaries. Lincoln's Inn also includes a few flats that are occupied by Bar students, the rent being part of these students' Inn scholarships.

The resemblance between the Inns and Oxford and Cambridge colleges is uncanny: the quadrangles, architecture, halls, and stairwells will put the **Oxbridge** student immediately at home. Those who have come from an old public school, through an **Oxbridge** college, to an Inn may well spend almost the entirety of their life in this tranquil (if homogenous) environment, although others should not have any problem in getting use to it. Charles Dickens, who did not enjoy his time in Gray's Inn (in South Square) and whose impression was in marked contrast to Hawthorne's (above), did not find it either tranquil or welcoming. He states (with reference to the buildings of the time that have since been destroyed in the Blitz):

> I look upon Gray's Inn generally as one of the most depressing institutions in brick and mortar, known to the children of men. Can anything be more dreary than its arid Square, Sahara Desert of the law, with the ugly old tiled-topped tenements, the dirty windows, the bills To Let, To Let, the door-posts inscribed like gravestones, the crazy gateway giving upon the filthy Lane, the scowling, iron-barred prison-like passage into Verulam buildings, the mouldy red-nosed ticket-porters with little coffin plates, and why with aprons, the dry, hard, atomy-like appearance of the whole dust-heap?

> (Dickens, *The Uncommercial Traveller* (London, Chapman & Hall, 1861),
> in chapter 14)

A further word should be said on what Dickens refers to as the 'door-posts inscribed like gravestones': all barristers' chambers have outside their front door an engraved plaque listing their current members in order of seniority (QCs first, and then juniors in decreasing order of years since **call**). It is difficult not to look wistfully at this plaque while walking through the front doors every day as a pupil.

As was earlier mentioned, a student must be admitted to one of the **Inns of Court** prior to registration on the BVC, although there is nothing to stop admission to an Inn before that (even years before). In the long run, it doesn't matter very much which Inn you join as you will spend most time in practice using the library and dining room of whichever Inn is nearest to your chambers, whether or not that is the Inn of which you are a member. As a student member, however, it does make some difference, as you will have to use your own Inn for the following things: the library; the **dining**; the **mooting**; and the **advocacy** training.

THE INN LIBRARIES

Apart from being a good place to check email for free, the Inn libraries are all better stocked than most university law libraries. They are all good-looking in their own way (don't forget to look up and gasp every now and again), although I prefer the nooks and crannies of Inner Temple Library and the bookishness of Lincoln's Inn Library to the two other Inn libraries. Students may only use the library in the Inn of which they are a member, although barristers (and pupils, and often mini-pupils) may use any, and will probably make frequent use of whichever Inn library is nearest to them and their chambers. All the Inn libraries subscribe to the major case reports and electronic resources and have the most oft-used textbooks, but they all also have various specialisms, which should maximise the chances that at least one Inn library has the book you are looking for. You can look on the web to see which Inn library specialises in which area. You can also find out which journals and law reports (from the UK and abroad) are available at which Inn by looking at http://www.innertemplelibrary. org.uk.

THE CHAPELS

Each Inn has its own chapel with a pastor who, as well as presiding over church services, may well have pastoral responsibilities for Inn members of all religions or none: generally, anyone is welcome in the chapels for a moment of reflection whether they are a believer or not, although the precise policy depends upon the particular chaplain. If your powers of advocacy stretch to persuading someone to marry you, your Inn chapel, and Inn reception rooms, make a rather grand option for a wedding venue.

WHEN AND HOW DO I JOIN?

You must join an Inn by May of the year prior to commencement of your **BVC**: you may accept a place on the BVC but you may not register on the course without being a member of an Inn. You may apply to join only one Inn at a time, and you may join only one Inn.[26] Application forms to join an Inn are available from the Inns or their websites (see the 'Further Information' section). The application fee is £85 at the time of writing. Assuming you have a referee (any responsible person who has known you for over a year) and are not a criminal, you shouldn't have any problem becoming a member.

You do not have to be a member of an Inn at the time you apply for one of the Inn's BVC scholarships, since you apply for these scholarships in the November before the BVC begins and the deadline for joining an Inn is six months later, in the May before the BVC. However as you may only apply for scholarships to one Inn, by applying you have in any event chosen your Inn once and for all.

The advantages of joining an Inn well before you apply for scholarships are as follows:

- It might impress the Inn as to your seriousness about coming to the Bar.
- When you are a member of an Inn, you can get advice and interview practice from your Inn's Education and Training Department and possibly work experience such as **judge shadowing**. Further, many Inns provide you with a mentor or **sponsor**, who is a barrister designated to advise you on applications and the like.
- Once you have joined an Inn you can start **dining** and doing your other **qualifying sessions** (see chapter nine), although for them to count towards your quota they cannot be more than two years before your **call** (in other words, more than one year before you start your BVC).
- The earlier you join, the nearer the front of the line you are at your **call** ceremony (not a huge advantage, this one!).

The disadvantages are:

- You may only apply to your own Inn for scholarships so you are committing yourself to that Inn and its scholarships by joining (although you'll have to pick one in any case eventually).
- If you decide not to become a barrister, you will have wasted your joining fee (about £85).

---

[26] This is not strictly true because as a more senior barrister you can become what is called an '*ad eundem* member' of a second Inn

CHOOSING

You cannot choose the wrong Inn. As Harold Morris observed over 70 years ago: 'The selection of an Inn of Court is more often than not a matter of chance; friendship with, or an introduction to, some member of the Bar being in most cases the deciding factor.' (*The Barrister* (London, Geoffrey Bles, 1930) p 14). This is still remarkably accurate. (I chose mine because I met an eminent public law QC at university who recommended his Inn. I joined the Inn, but then later became interested in commercial law and have not seen the eminent QC since.) What most people don't realise is that your chambers is nothing to do with the Inn you are a member of. Even if you are in a London chambers situated in an Inn, most of the members of your chambers will (as a matter of luck) not be members of that Inn because they all joined an Inn before they knew which chambers they were going to (although they will use the library and dining room of the Inn they are located in, for convenience).

Things to bear in mind when choosing include the following (and I should declare my interest now: I am a member of Gray's):

- which you like the look of;
- the size of the Inn (Gray's is smaller, which means that if you are a member of Gray's you are more likely to get to know other students at **dinners**, since it is a smaller group that dines, but you will meet fewer people in Bar school and elsewhere who are members of your Inn). The **amount** of scholarship money available is broadly proportionate to the size of the Inn, so there is no advantage to be gained there;
- the types of scholarships available: if you're a brilliant candidate you may want an Inn with a few really big awards; if you're not you may prefer an Inn that has a larger number of smaller awards. The big Lincoln's Inn awards include the option of accommodation in the Inn. Gray's Inn is the only one to offer large merit-based awards during the pupillage year as well as during the BVC year (although not many);
- Gray's Inn and Lincoln's Inn are nearer to the Inns of Court School of Law than the other two Inns;
- the standard of advocacy training (all are good but Gray's is understood to be a market leader, with a full day's trial in the **Royal Courts of Justice** in front of a real judge);

- the standard and price of the food (Lincoln's has good fish and chips on Fridays);
- the quality of other societies and entertainments such as drama, music, mooting, and debating;
- the dining events and speakers;
- the quality of the other amenities (Gray's Inn has a fairly horrible café-bar, Middle Temple has a pub with views over the lawns, Inner Temple and Lincoln's have smart cocktail bars with fairly good food), although you can use these whichever Inn you are a member of;
- how nice the Student Officer is;
- whether the Inn provides a mentoring scheme and will help you with your pupillage applications;
- whether the Inn has particular links with your university or Bar school;
- whether you like the feel of the library (although this only really applies to your BVC year because once you are a barrister you will use the library nearest to your chambers, whether that of another Inn if you are in London, or another library if you are on **circuit**);
- I'm sure they are all good at this, but I've heard that Middle is particularly good at making those doing the BVC outside London feel welcome.

To help you choose, you should certainly look around the Inns and go to speakto the Student Officer at each Inn that interests you. Spend some time looking at their websites too: *www.graysinn.org.uk*, *www.innertemple.org.uk*, *www.lincolnsinn. org.uk*, *www.middletemple. org.uk*.

SCHOLARSHIPS

Between them, the Inns offer about £2.5 million of funding for BVC students. The deadline is the November before the BVC (see the next chapter).

8

The BVC

ABOUT THE BAR VOCATIONAL COURSE

Attempts have been made, by means of glossy brochures, to sell the **BVC** (and the solicitors' equivalent, the **LPC** or **Legal Practice Course**) as a course that qualifies its students for a variety of careers. While it is true that the skills learned on the BVC are to some extent transferable, it is also true that (given the cost of the BVC) it is not recommended for those who are not firmly decided upon a career at the Bar (or as an equivalent advocate abroad). The vast majority of BVC graduates who are not barristers or practising abroad are those who didn't get a suitable pupillage or tenancy or who decided that they did not want to be a barrister after all. It is a rare few who always intended the BVC as a stepping stone to a different career (although the moves by some BVC providers to make it into a master's degree, discussed below, go some way to giving it value as a stand-alone qualification).

The form and content of the BVC is a matter of some controversy and is constantly evolving. As it currently stands, it is (in my opinion) an over-expensive, fairly well-taught course in which the student learns legal skills over eight to ten months full time or over two years part time (the latter taking place either in the evenings or at weekends, depending upon the course). The BVC does not teach law, other than procedural and evidential law; rather it teaches professional ethics and the practical skills of drafting, opinion-writing, advocacy, negotiation, case preparation, and client interviewing, by means of lectures, seminars, and performance sessions (often including critical analysis of the video playback of a student's performance).

However, in a recent consultation at the end of 2005, the **Bar Council** mooted the possibility of introducing more law into the BVC and possibly trying to turn it into a master's degree. A couple of BVC providers have jumped ahead in this respect, and their BVC students have the option of applying to combine their BVC with an **LLM** in advanced legal practice (or a similar term). Following completion of their BVC, and completion (during the BVC year or the following year) of a supervised dissertation on an area of legal practice and procedure, the students will be granted an LLM in addition to their BVC. Currently this option is available at the Inns of Court School of Law and Northumbria University, and the extra LLM fees cost around £2,000. The Inns of Court School of Law LLM programme is currently only for those doing their BVC at that institution, whereas the Northumbria programme is available to those who have done a BVC elsewhere. For more information on the content of the BVC courses, see the Bar Council's brochure on the BVC (for the relevant contact address see the 'Further Information' section at the end of the book) and the websites of the relevant institutions that provide the BVC (listed later in this chapter).

The skills that are taught on the BVC are not easy to teach, but it is fair to say that the BVC has come under a lot of criticism. Whether or not the criticism is justified, it is clear that, at least as it presently stands, barristers in the chambers to which you may be applying for pupillage will probably want you to have been graded 'Very Competent' or 'Outstanding' on the BVC (yes, the BVC is graded according to a scale you will last have encountered at primary school), although this grade is certainly not as important as your degree class.

THE COST OF THE BVC

In 2006/07 the average cost of the BVC course (including books, but not including any living costs) was £12,000 in London, £9,000 outside London, with the part-time course totalling a very similar amount over the two years of its duration. There is a Bar Council registration fee of £300 on top of that.

The average scholarship received by a BVC student from his or her **Inn** is between £1,000 and £2,000 and most get much less (because, given these averages, for every student with a £12,000 scholarship there are about seven with nothing or next to nothing).

The cost of the BVC is high. There are rumours that some local education authorities will fund the BVC, but in general there is no funding available, and as the course is not academic the usual academic funding bodies are not interested. Bar funding is a matter of some controversy, because barristers realise that the future of the Bar depends upon it having the cream of the legal crop, and many strong candidates are deterred from the Bar (and often become solicitors) because of the financial difficulties they would face trying to get to the Bar. Things are getting better (a few years ago there was no minimum pupillage award and so some pupils were paid nothing), but the situation is still fairly dire for Bar students. The following are the major sources of funding.[27]

1) Self-funding and Loans

Most funding comes within this category: savings, earnings from part-time jobs during the BVC, money from generous relatives, and loans. Given that most BVC students will already be in debt, this is the reason for the disproportionate middle- and upper-class contingents at the Bar. As far as loans are concerned, they fall into two main types: professional studies loans and Career Development Loans.[28]

Professional studies loans/professional trainee loans for the BVC (or, in many cases, for the CPE/GDL or LLM) of up to £25,000 are currently offered by NatWest, HSBC, Lloyds/TSB, Barclays and the Royal Bank of Scotland, with repayments often deferred until six months to two years after the course has finished (although interest accrues from day one) and with a repayment period of up to ten years. Interest is charged at fairly reasonable rates, currently around 7–8 per cent, and in some cases a student account with interest-free overdraft is also available. See the relevant banks' websites for details.

Career Development Loans are sponsored by the government, which pays the interest for the duration of the course, and are currently offered by Barclays, the Co-operative Bank and the Royal Bank of Scotland for up to £8,000 (which doesn't even cover the BVC course fees). When the course finishes, however, interest accrues at pretty high rates, currently at between 10 and 18 per cent, and you will have

---

[27] Further information can be found at http://legal education.org.uk/downloads/finance.doc.

[28] Note that, unfortunately, student loans from the Student Loans Company are not available for the BVC.

between one and five years to repay (the interest rate and repayment period depending upon the bank and how much you have borrowed).[29]

2) Scholarships from Inns of Court

These are all tax free, and range from one hundred pounds to cover the cost of membership of the Inn up to £20,000 for the year (at least half of which would go on BVC fees). You may only apply to the Inn of which you are a member or have applied to become a member. Between them, at the time of going to press, the four Inns of Court provided £2.5 million per year to Bar school students. The criteria for awarding the scholarships vary from Inn to Inn and scholarship to scholarship. Generally speaking, there is a significant focus on merit, with key factors in applications being prizes, mooting, and coming across as bright and clued-up in the interview. Means (ie the extent of your financial need) will also be relevant to some scholarships or to the amount of the award you are given. The deadlines for applications are usually at the end of the October before the BVC. Every year a large number of people who would have got scholarships fail to apply for them either through ignorance, undervaluing their chances, or missing the deadlines. You have nothing to lose. Nevertheless, you would be foolish to assume that you will get a scholarship and sensible to assume the opposite (perhaps allowing you to be pleasantly surprised).

4) Early Draw-down of Pupillage Awards

Even if you have a pupillage lined up when you start the BVC, your chambers will not fund your BVC (in stark contrast to solicitors' firms, which pay for the **LPC** in addition to paying a salary to trainees), although a few of the richer chambers will allow a significant proportion of the pupillage award (often up to £10,000) to be drawn down early to assist with funding the BVC year. The Mountfield Report in 2002 proposed that barristers earning over £100,000 pay a 0.25 per cent levy on earnings to fund BVC students, but this report was shelved in the face of strong opposition. A more recent report has proposed a fund taking voluntary contributions

---

[29] For more information on Career Development Loans and links to the relevant banks see www.direct.gov.uk/cdl.

from barristers, although at the time of writing this had not been implemented. As discussed above in chapter one, a small number of the organisations that make up the **Employed Bar** and that offer pupillages will pay for the BVC as well.

5) Essay Prizes

There are law essay prizes out there, and, like pupillage awards, they are very good for the CV as well as the wallet. Such competitions are often, perhaps unsurprisingly, undersubscribed (I've heard of there being less than a handful of entrants to essay competitions paying out over a thousand pounds to the winner and several hundred to the runner up). The principal organisers of such competitions are the Inns, whose annual competitions are generally open only to their members (prize money for the essay competitions ranges from a couple of hundred pounds up to £1,500), but the Bar Council also runs an annual law reform essay competition (top prize £2,500: see the Bar Council's website), and there are others such as the Outer Temple Chambers £3,000 Calcutt prize (www.outertemple.com/prize.php) (for others keep your eyes on the Inns of Court notice boards and the pages of **Counsel**, the Bar Council's magazine, and the broadsheets). These things are worth entering, and even if you don't win, you may well be able to turn your essay into an article and get it published in a law journal, adding more CV points.

6) Other

There may be other funding out there—see the finances factsheet on the Bar Council website. (The only other large scholarship I've come across is from Oxford University: if you have a first from Oxford you can apply for the £6,500 Eldon Law Scholarship to help with BVC funding. The deadline is October: go and see the Secretary to the Oxford Law Faculty in the St Cross Building or a do a Google search).

7) Tax Back

If you write the cheque for the BVC yourself (rather than eg your parents doing so), and keep the invoice, you may well be able to effectively claim a few thousand of it back as a tax deduction later.

WHERE TO DO THE BVC

It used only to be possible to study the BVC in London at the Inns of Court School of Law, but now it is taught at a variety of places throughout England and Wales. The following BVC providers are, at the time of writing, properly accredited to provide the BVC. Up-to-date information is available from http://www.barstandardsboard.org.uk.

BPP Law School	London Leeds	full-time or part-time (evenings)	http://www.bpp.com/law/
Cardiff University	Cardiff	full-time only	http://www.law.cf.ac.uk/cpls/bvc
College of Law	London	full-time or part-time (weekends)	http://www.college-of-law.co.uk
Inns of Court School of Law (part of City University)	London	full-time or part-time (evenings)	http://www.city.ac.uk/icsl
Manchester Metropolitan University	Manchester	full-time only	http://www.law.mmu.ac.uk/ postgrad/bvc/
Nottingham Trent University	Nottingham	full-time only	http://www.ntu.ac.uk/nls/ professional_courses/bvc
University of West England	Bristol	full-time or part-time (weekends)	http://bilp.uwe.ac.uk/bvc
University of Northumbria	Newcastle	full-time only	http://northumbria.ac.uk/sd/ academic/law/

All the BVC providers are validated by the **Bar Standards Board**, and the course content is largely laid down by the Board. Partly because of this, the BVC providers do not differ in quality or reputation as much as university law departments do, so the place where one studied the BVC is unlikely to make much direct difference to chances of getting pupillage.

Relevant factors in choosing where to do the BVC include:

- where you are going to practise (this is relevant because you may get links to chambers or a **circuit** through the lecturers or through your **Inn** activities during the year);
- the London BVC providers are, of course, close to the Inns of Court (particularly the Inns of Court School of Law and BPP, which are walking distance away) and so this makes it easier to use the Inn

facilities and to do the requisite number of **dining** sessions. Just as importantly, if you don't have a pupillage lined up when you finish the BVC you may want to go to your Inn officers for advice, but if you have a full-time job outside London while you are looking for pupillage you will not easily be able to visit your Inn, and your Inn's knowledge of the local situations outside London will be limited;

- the London BVCs cost about £3,000 more than the others, and London living costs are higher;
- although all the BVCs include the same basic subjects, not all the BVCs offer the same range of optional courses (often referred to as 'electives'), and some courses are offered by only one BVC provider;
- the BVC providers do not use identical teaching methods. Some of them focus more on lectures; others more on small-group sessions. Not all examine in the same way either (eg most but not all of them use multiple-choice-tests to examine some parts of the course);
- Not all the BVC providers have the same **pro bono** opportunities (eg advice clinics, **FRU**) etc and not all have the same tradition of getting involved with (and winning) **mooting** competitions;
- If you do the **GDL** and BVC at the College of Law then you will get an **LLB** undergraduate degree in law (as was explained in chapter five). If you do the BVC at the Inns of Court School of Law or Northumbria University, you can also get an **LLM** by completing a suitable supervised dissertation (as was explained earlier in this chapter), although students who complete their BVC elsewhere can also do the LLM afterwards at Northumbria.

Chambers & Partners provides a useful table comparing the various BVCs: see www.chambersandpartners.com/chambersstudent. You can also get the brochures and speak to representatives of the course providers at law fairs (which often also have talks about careers at the Bar etc). All of the BVC providers have open days, which are well worth going to.

GETTING ONTO THE BVC AND THINKING TWICE

To get onto the BVC you need a 2:2 honours degree (although there is talk of toughening up the requirement).

The BVC applications system is run through BVC Online (www.bvconline. co.uk) and is conducted by application form only, that is, there are no interviews. It currently costs £40 to apply, and the success rate for applicants is somewhere in the region of 60 per cent, or a little higher. Applications are made to three BVC providers (which you list in order of preference) approximately a year before commencement of the course, according to the following timetable (although for the precise dates check the relevant website):

October before the BVC begins	You may start applying for a BVC
November before the BVC begins	Deadline for Inns of Court scholarship applications
January before the BVC begins	Deadline for BVC applications
March before the BVC begins	Offers are made to BVC applicants
March to April before the BVC begins	Inn scholarship interviews
March to July before the BVC begins	BVC clearing pool (you can make your first BVC application in this pool but it is not recommended to wait until this point)
May	Deadline for joining an Inn
September	BVC begins
June after the course begins	Full-time BVC ends (or one year later for the part-time course)

The online application form is mainly concerned with your educational and work history. It also includes one page in which you must write a maximum 4,096 characters under each of the following headings: 'Mini-pupillages and other Bar-related experience', 'Reasons for choice of career', 'Evidence of intellectual ability', 'Inter-personal skills', 'Advocacy and public speaking', and 'Personal organisational skills'. You do not have to complete the form all in one go, and it is best to draft each answer carefully on paper or in your word processor, and then cut and paste it into the box in the BVC Online form once you have edited it and checked it for spelling and other errors. Do not rush this, consider every sentence to decide whether it is saying something useful, is in the right place, and is saying what you want to say in the best and clearest way possible. You can save the different pages and return to them on another day, but once you have submitted it to the system you cannot change any of your answers.

Those applying to the BVC should realise that this is the crunch point when you are committing to the Bar. The Office of Fair Trading has said that the Bar is not allowed to put a restriction on numbers taking the BVC, which means that there are far more places available on the BVC than there are pupillages. It is therefore vital that students understand that their being accepted onto a BVC course is no guarantee of pupillage, and only between a quarter and third of those who do the BVC (and pay the ten grand or so) will ever get pupillage (see the statistics at the start of chapter five). Many or most chambers offer pupillages over a year in advance. If you do not wait until you have a pupillage lined up, and do not have a large Inn scholarship (discussed above), but still do the BVC in the hope of getting pupillage later, you should be aware that you are taking a big risk. Whether you do so is up to you, but if you do then make sure it is with your eyes open. There are far too many students on the BVC who have a good chance of passing the course (the pass rate is pretty high) but have almost no chance of getting pupillage (because their academic background, intelligence, and advocacy skills are not up to par), a fact that is evident to everyone except those students themselves.

THE BVC YEAR

Unless you are inefficient (and many BVC students are), even doing just about all the work given to you on the BVC will not take all your time (I would estimate that three fairly full 9 am–6 pm days per week are ample, although many of the courses require attendance on four days per week). Given the cost of the course, a part-time job may be a fruitful way of filling up any spare time (and your bank account), and any other time should be spent doing the activities set out below in order to boost your CV and your experience.

One of the things you absolutely must do during this year is **mooting** (discussed above in chapter five). If you haven't done any at university, now is the time to start. If you have, now is the time to continue. There may be some mooting organised through your Bar School, but most will take place in or through your Inn, often in front of real Court of Appeal judges and 50 or more of your fellow student members of the Inn. Nevertheless, the experience is very useful, the CV points are more than handy, the opportunity to chat and get feedback from real judges is invaluable, and if you're too scared or lazy to moot, then what are you doing trying to be a barrister? Hassle your Inn student officer or Master of Moots or whoever is responsible for mooting.

Other things to do might include:

• *The Inn Advocacy Weekends.* Your Inn will run optional advocacy weekends (eg the ones at Cumberland Lodge that you might hear of). As well as being a good way of getting a few **qualifying sessions** out of the way (see the next chapter), they provide an unparalleled way of getting to know some barristers, QCs, and judges very well and improving your advocacy through very well-designed exercises and individual feedback from experts.

• *Debating.* This is parliamentary-style argument on (usually) non-legal topics, and you can do it through your Inn. This can also be good practice and (so I'm told) good fun. Although often the people who debate in their Inn are the people who have debated before, at least some of the Inns run beginners courses and workshops.

• *Essay competitions and articles.* Enter legal essay competitions (see above). You may want to write something for a law journal, perhaps a case note or even a full article. It needn't be for the highest profile journals (the *Law Quarterly Review* etc) as there are plenty of lower-rank journals and student journals that are less competitive, although if you think you've done a good piece of work then there's no reason why the top-rank journals won't publish it. These are also good for CV points, and help to convince chambers that you know what you're talking about (ie the law) and are genuinely interested in it.

• *Jobs and pro bono.* You will almost certainly have time to do some unpaid legal assistance volunteering, or even some part-time paid legal jobs, as set out in chapter six. This stuff is great for your CV.

During the BVC a student will primarily use the library of his or her Bar school and the library of his or her own Inn. I would advise using the latter if it is sufficiently conveniently located: it is likely to have the Bar manuals and all the books that the Bar school will have but they will be in far less demand and it will be far quieter. A BVC student is not entitled to use the libraries of the Inns of Court of which he or she is not a member.

Also, a pretty good lunch is available in your Inn for not too much money (students and pupils are subsidised), and, although I understand that wearing shorts is not allowed, you don't have to dress smartly.

9

Dining, Qualifying Sessions, and Call

THE QUALIFYING SESSIONS

Before **call**, in addition to completing the BVC, a student must do the requisite number of **qualifying sessions** at his or her **Inn**, currently 12. These sessions are usually of the following types (although not all Inns offer all of the following):

- an *introductory session* where there are a few talks welcoming you to the Inn and telling you what it can do for you and what you can do for it;
- *dinners*. The lion's share of most people's qualifying sessions will be taken up with dinners, as discussed below;
- the occasional *Sunday lunch*;
- *Inn weekends*, for example at Cumberland Lodge in Windsor Great Park, Berkshire (often worth three qualifying units);
- *'special education days'* for non-London students, which make it possible for non-London students to accumulate several qualifying sessions in one visit to London. These usually include a lunch, a qualifying dinner, and a seminar or two, and count for several units;
- *call night* (the night of your **call** to the Bar)—obviously this won't count if you take the option of being **called** in *absentia*: that is, without appearing at the ceremony.

If you think twelve qualifying sessions is a demanding number, think about the students in the seventeenth century, who had to dine for 12 <u>terms</u>; the qualifying sessions are the modern equivalent of **keeping terms**, the residence requirements of student barristers in prior centuries when the Inns were residential law schools. Indeed, dining still takes place during the Inn's four 'terms', which are about a month long and run (approximately) in January, April, June, and November. These used to be the court terms as well, although court sittings are now on a different calendar entirely.

You can complete your qualifying sessions at any time after joining the Inn providing it is within two years before your call, although it is normal to do most or all during the BVC year.

DINING

Although there are a few other types of qualifying session, the most common qualifying session is the **dinner**: my 12 units were made up of 10 dinners throughout the year of my BVC, with the other two being the introductory session and call night.

For a dinner to count as a qualifying session, the student usually also has to attend an edifying event that precedes or succeeds the dinner (sometimes called the *domus*, Latin for 'home', part of the evening). This might be a moot before dinner, or a talk, debate, drama, or musical recital after dinner. This is all by way of taking part in the life of the Inn—your professional club—and there is a long history of such entertainment and socialising.

The dinners themselves are governed by fairly arcane rules, many of which are common to all dinners at all Inns:

- Everyone wears a gown during dinner. The Inns lend you student gowns on the night, and as they are different to barristers' gowns (being without sleeves), it would be foolish to buy one).
- As at many formal dinners, grace is said (briefly) in Latin before and after the meal.
- Students are not permitted to leave the hall during dinner, whether to go to the toilet or otherwise. If they wish to do so, they must request permission from the Treasurer or other senior member present, generally by passing her or him a note. Given the amount of wine consumed, this rule can sometimes lead to a stressful evening.
- Everyone is seated at long tables but is a part of a **mess** of four, which means a group of four people comprising two pairs opposite each other on either side of the table. Dining in messes was common to all banquets in bygone days, but now happens rarely outside the

Inns and parts of the military. The mess system also includes obligatory toasting, as Harold Morris observes:

> There is an ancient courtesy when the wine is opened. The members of the Mess drink the health of one another, and then the whole Mess drinks the health of the Mess dining on each side of them.
>
> (*The Barrister* (London, Geoffrey Bles, 1930) p 20)

This toasting continues to the present day, but you will soon get the hang of it and it is a good way of getting to know the names of those dining nearby.

Not everyone is a fan of Inn dining. At its worst, dining is as described by Charles Dickens in the following terms:

> I myself was uncommercially preparing for the Bar—which is done, as everybody knows, by having a frayed old gown put on in a pantry by an old woman in a chronic state of Saint Anthony's fire and dropsy and, so decorated, bolting a bad dinner in a party of four, whereof each individual mistrusts the other three.
>
> (Dickens, *The Uncommercial Traveller* (London, Chapman & Hall, 1861), chapter 14)

You should also be aware that each dinner will cost upwards of about £12 (special dinners cost more than ordinary evenings), so this too must be factored into your budget.

CALL TO THE BAR

The **call** to the Bar is a ceremony in the Inn in either spring or autumn, or at the start or the end of the summer. During the call, each student processes through the hall of his Inn, in front of his or her parents and admirers, and is granted the status of barrister and the degree of **barrister-at-law**. This requires full dress (gown and **bands** etc) although it may be wise just to borrow them if you are not likely to need them in practice for a while (and so don't want to cough up the money now). Essentially, this is a graduation.

As JH Baker, the eminent legal historian, observes of those called to the Bar:

> They are not being admitted into practise, because that is a separate and unceremonious process, with its own increasingly complex regulation.

They are undertaking something more sublime, more than just the chance of earning a living: they are receiving a degree of learning in the law of the land.

> (*The Common Law Tradition: Lawyers, Books and the Law* (London, Hambledon Continuum, 1999))

This historical position is reflected by the current practice at the time of writing whereby the call ceremony takes place after successful completion of the BVC and is a necessary prerequisite to completion of pupillage, but does not of itself indicate the right to practise as a barrister.

However, the confusion engendered by a separation of those with the degree of barrister-at-law and those who are entitled to practise as a barrister has been noticed, and there are moves to change things. The Bar Council has recently approved **deferred call** proposals under which barristers will be called only once they have completed their full 12 months of pupillage, although they will be granted a **temporary call** after the **first six** as a technicality to entitle them to practise during their **second six**. The deferred call system would mean that those who have completed a BVC but not a pupillage would not be entitled to call themselves barristers, although it is already the case that such people cannot practise as barristers. At their earliest, the proposals may be implemented so as to affect those starting their BVC in autumn 2008, but they still require approval by the **Bar Standards Board** before they can be implemented (it is due to decide in summer 2007) and, given significant opposition to the proposals, may well yet be scrapped or delayed. These proposals are particularly worrying for Commonwealth students, who come to England to do the BVC in order to go home to practise as a lawyer but with the title of barrister. The deferred call system, if approved, may make exception for these students.

Call costs about £75, and you have to apply to your Inn with a passport photograph and references in good time.

10

Getting Pupillage

INTRODUCTION

By way of fairly recent example, in 2004, 1,251 people passed the **BVC**, whereas in the same year only 556 **pupillages** were available. Of course, the 1,251 people who passed in 2004 were not only competing with each other for a pupillage, they were also competing with most of the 600 BVC graduates who did not get a pupillage in autumn 2003, as well as who knows how many from 2002. As you can see, competition is fierce.

One resource that should be mentioned up-front is the **Inn** sponsorship scheme. Under this scheme (which does not involve sponsorship in a financial sense) your Inn will allocate a barrister to act as an adviser and mentor to each student member who wants one. At best, this **sponsor** will be in your intended area of practice and will be willing and able to give you advice, although do as much research as you can before you ask them, as they are busy people.

IMPROVING YOUR CHANCES

As has already been mentioned, the best way to improve your chances is to get a first or upper second-class degree at university. But it is also important to have other things on your CV that show that you are bright, active, and independent. Directly relevant activities such as working in **pro bono** advice clinics, **mooting**, or debating are excellent (mooting, in particular, is of the utmost importance—see further chapter five), but activities that are not so obviously relevant are almost as good: sailing, playing in an orchestra, being on your university or local hockey team, being involved with various committees and student unions, or doing real jobs with real responsibilities. As a barrister you will have to manage cases and people independently and this requires good people skills, common sense, and charisma. If you haven't done anything in life then you are unlikely to have these things. Of course, by the time you read this chapter it may be too late to do these things . . .

IN CHAMBERS OR ELSEWHERE

The vast majority of pupillages are in chambers, and even those who want to work at the **Employed Bar** will generally do their pupillage in a chambers, so there is, in practice, not much of a choice between chambers and elsewhere for the purpose of pupillage. However there are a few organisations, notably the **GLS**, that not only employ barristers but also train them through their own pupillage scheme. See further the discussion in chapter one.

CHOOSING YOUR AREA OF PRACTICE

Although many **chambers** cover a fairly wide range of practice areas, you will have to have some idea of what sort of chambers you want to go to in order to apply to the Bar. This is not least because some specialised chambers might not look at you if you show signs of being unsure that you want to take up their specialism (eg because the list of chambers you've applied to is all over the place, or your history of mini-pupillages shows no signs of recently focusing in on a specialism).

You will probably have had an idea of what sort of a barrister you want to be at the same time as deciding you want to be a barrister at all. There are three main types of reason why you might want to work in a chambers with a particular specialism.

(i)   You like a particular area of law.
(ii)   You want to work in a particular field of society, with a particular type of people (eg you'd rather be involved with personal

problems and cross-examine social workers about signs of abuse or husbands about their earnings, or you'd rather deal with technical problems and cross-examine builders about the depth of their foundations or doctors about the seriousness of a metatarsal fracture).[30]

(iii) You prefer the lifestyle that goes with certain areas of practice: you don't want to be led by **silks** very much (so you aren't keen on some commercial sets); you don't want to work with upsetting cases (so you aren't keen on the criminal or family Bars) or perhaps you want to work with real people and human problems (so you are keen on the criminal or family Bars); you want to get rich fairly quickly (so the legally aided Bar, particularly the criminal Bar, may not be for you);[31] you want to be on your feet most days (so pointing to the criminal and family and general common law Bars) or, on the contrary, spend the vast majority of your time on written work (the tax and Chancery Bars); or perhaps you want to spend quite a lot of your time researching intellectually challenging legal points (mainly the commercial, Chancery and tax Bars).

Whilst the 'A Week in the Life' chapter in this book[32] may have helped you to decide on an area of practice, there is some excellent information on the www.doctorjob.com/barrister and www.chambersandpartners/chambersstudent websites, setting out frank profiles of the different areas under the 'Essential Information' part of the page.

CHOOSING THE GEOGRAPHICAL LOCATION

This basically means: do you want to be a barrister in London or elsewhere? London **pupillage awards** are generally higher, but then the cost of living in London is higher than elsewhere and to live in affordable accommodation may require a fairly long daily commute. Most of the very specialised sets (such as commercial, tax, human rights, chancery) are in London, and so most of the cases in those fields go to the barristers there, but if you want to go to a chambers that does

---

[30] See further the discussion in chapter one.
[31] If you do want to practise in the areas of work that are legally aided then it is perhaps advisable to go to a set that also does other privately funded work, in order to help your cash flow along in the tough early years.
[32] Chapter three.

mixed work or a criminal or family set, then the sets outside London are likely to be just as good as those in London, with the advantages of being on the whole less competitive and often more friendly (because the **circuits** are smaller communities of barristers than the London community, although bear in mind that London is a part of the South Eastern circuit). Barristers outside London may find a dearth of cases in their preferred field and have to do work that is below their level of experience, but on the other hand they may find that cases come to them that are above their level because there is no one else suited to the case in the area. However there are increasing amounts of commercial, chancery, and other work outside London, and so nowadays you will find successful specialised sets in these fields too in the major cities (particularly Manchester and Leeds, but also Liverpool, Birmingham, Newcastle, and Cardiff).

CHOOSING YOUR CHAMBERS

The pupillages website (www.pupillages.com) and the accompanying *Pupillages and Awards Handbook* (available for free from the Bar Council) will be your central reference guide. There is also the rival (not as good for barristers) *Training Contract and Pupillages Handbook*, published under the supervision of the **Law Society**, and available from careers centres or www.tcph.co.uk. The **Code of Conduct** requires all **first six** and **second six** pupillages in chambers (but not **third six** pupillages) to be advertised on the Bar Council's website at www.pupillages.com, and while everything on there should be up to date, you should also cross-refer to the chambers' own website and brochure, as there have been occasions of chambers forgetting to update their information (number of pupillages, deadlines, etc) on the central website.

You can also use the bigger directories of chambers such as the *Bar Directory*, *Chambers & Partners UK Edition*, and the Legal 500. These will be available in many (although not all) local libraries and career centres, otherwise go to your city's central library or, if you've joined an Inn, your Inn library. These directories provide rankings and descriptions of chambers and how they are doing.

Unfortunately, brochures and websites tell you very little in their blurbs to distinguish them from each other. (If I see another job advertisement asking for 'dynamic people', I might lose my mind: what jobs do static people do?) However, if you look carefully enough, you can get useful information from them, such as the number of **silks** and the major cases argued by members of chambers (some of which cases you will know about from your legal studies or the legal press). Compare and contrast. Work out what is important to you and work out which chambers offer those things. Draw up tables if that helps. Very useful is the Chambers & Partners website, which includes no-nonsense descriptions of what pupillage is like at various chambers and their history of how many pupils have been taken on: www.chambersandpartners.com/chambersstudent. Your best information will come from talking to your Inn **sponsor** (if you have one) and barristers and other applicants at **dinners** and other **Inn** events, on mini-pupillages, and at Bar school.

If you possibly can, you really should also attend the National Pupillage Fair in March and talk to barristers and pick up brochures. Information is available at http://www.doctorjob.com/law/fair/. It is by far the best way of getting to talk to and ask questions of barristers at the various chambers, as well as picking up all the brochures in one place. Dress as you would for an interview, because some of the chambers might take notice of such things.

Some criteria to take into account when choosing chambers include the following:

(i) *The fields of practice of the members of chambers.* Although it is possible to develop your practice in fields outside those of your chambers, in reality you will have little control over your specialisms in the early years so will end up doing whatever comes to you, and the work that comes to you is the work that the chambers regularly does.

(ii) *The location of the chambers.* Getting pupillage at chambers outside central London is likely to be easier because it is less competitive than getting pupillage in central London.

(iii) *The reputation and standard of the chambers.* This works both ways: if you are not a superstar candidate there is no point in applying for a superstar set, particularly through **OLPAS**, where you have only a limited number of chambers to which you can apply. Look at the CVs of the people at the junior end of the chambers as an indicator of the quality of their (successful) pupils: if you don't think you can compete because they have far more prizes or experience than you then you may find it hard to shine when you are a pupil alongside such people (although, of course, there is a lot that you can't tell from a CV). If your application for a mini-pupillage has been rejected then, unless something changes on your CV, there is little point in applying for a pupillage (especially if it wastes one of your 12 OLPAS chambers)—this is a good way of testing the waters. It is important, however, not to focus on league tables such as in the Legal 500 to the exclusion of all other factors. Providing a chambers is of sufficient standing, its pupils and junior tenants will get high quality cases on the strength of the chambers' reputation, and there will be opportunities to work with and learn from good people. Ultimately, a barrister's career will depend upon his or her own ability, and there are stars in mediocre chambers and mediocre barristers in star chambers, so don't worry about whether a chambers is sixth rather than second on a league table. If your chambers is good enough, you will shine if you deserve to, so think of the reputation and standard of chambers more as a threshold that you want your chambers to pass than as an overriding factor.

(iv)   *The ratio of **silks** to **juniors***. A high ratio may indicate that there will be a good reputation, lots of **junioring** work, and a keenness to fill the bottom end of the chambers by taking on more tenants (since silks need juniors on their cases, and their links with solicitors bring smaller work into chambers for juniors to do). Nevertheless, in many areas of law there are fewer silks (because more barristers become judges, there is less work for silks in such areas, fewer bother applying for silk, or fewer are granted silk) and so you should only compare the number of silks among chambers in the same area of the country and the law.

(v)   *The feel of the chambers*: friendly; young or old; skewed or equally balanced between the sexes; modern or old fashioned. Examine the website, noting the gender balance and the background of the barristers (which universities, what prior careers), although note that the website's glossiness and content may be as much about the marketing budget as about the true ethos of the chambers. Most information, however, can be gleaned only by doing **mini-pupillages**, talking to members of chambers at law fairs, and swapping information with other people making applications or already in chambers. If you can get a feel for what the **clerks** are like, that is also important: in some chambers the clerks will pressure junior barristers if the clerks feel the juniors are not working hard enough or are taking too many holidays, whereas in others the clerks don't see that as part of their role and so the barristers get to enjoy more of the freedom that being self-employed affords.

(vi) *The number of pupils and the number of offers of* **tenancy** *made each year.* This is very important, and in essence it is an indicator of how good your chances of tenancy are: Two out of three? One out of four? (Although, of course, it is not a matter of simple chance.) The numbers may vary from year to year but there will be a general trend, and you are entitled to ask people in chambers (or in interview or after you've been offered a pupillage) what the past history is. If there are lots of years with no pupils taken on, and no explanation is forthcoming, then you should be worried that people are being rejected for reasons other than merit (politics? a fear that there is no work for juniors? pupils used as cheap labour?). Don't simply believe a chambers when it says that it will grant pupillage only to serious candidates and that it will take as many tenants as are good enough—just about all chambers say that. Actions speak louder than words.

(vii) *The destination of pupils who didn't get tenancy.* This is another important factor as it indicates how much effort the chambers expended in using its contacts to find a **third six** elsewhere for pupils who didn't get tenancy. If former pupils left the Bar that may (although won't necessarily) indicate that pupillage at that chambers was horrible. Again, you are perfectly entitled to ask chambers for this information at interview or after you've been offered a pupillage—put them in the hot-seat for a change—although, of course, don't be too cocky or aggressive.

(viii) *Size of the* pupillage award (see below).

(ix) *The buildings.* Many chambers are reaching the capacity of their current buildings and this may make them more cautious when considering whether to take on new tenants. Conversely, a chambers that has just expanded into a new building or annexe may be keen to fill some more rooms and get some rent, and so be slightly less choosy as regards its new tenants.

One factor to ignore is your Inn. Even if you are a member of Lincoln's Inn (for example), and you are applying to a London chambers, that provides no reason to apply or not to apply to the chambers physically located in Lincoln's Inn.

FIRST SIX PLUS SECOND SIX EQUALS TWELVE MONTHS

Most pupillages offered by a chambers are now for the full 12 months of pupillage, but some are for six months (requiring you to do a **first six** in one set and a **second six** in another). Further, some 12-month pupillages guarantee that the pupils will be permitted to stay for the full 12 months and complete their pupillage, whereas other chambers offering a 12-month pupillage have a 'culling point' after six months or possibly some other period when they may decide that some of their pupils are not good enough and terminate the pupillage, in effect turning it into a first six pupillage. See further the discussion above in chapter one.

PUPILLAGE AWARDS

> Since 2003, all chambers have been required to pay **pupillage awards** (or to guarantee earnings) at a monthly rate equivalent to £10,000 per year, plus travel from chambers to courts and other places, plus compulsory training courses. The top commercial and **Chancery** sets pay a pupillage award of up to £50,000 for a 12-month pupillage, with the pupil likely to earn some money on top of this during the **second six**.

Twenty years ago pupils had to pay pupil supervisors. The establishment of a minimum pupillage award is a recent and, on the whole, welcome development (see further the discussion in chapter two). Pupillage awards are rising every year, and while the top commercial chambers are paying more than commercial solicitors' firms (in order to prevent the best and brightest being drained to the firms), that is £40,000 to £50,000, the majority of criminal and other sets currently pay between £10,000 and £15,000. This is not a lot of money, and will barely cover rent in London.

Further, chambers are permitted to offset some of the award by the pupil's **second six** earnings. The default position is that the chambers must pay at least £833.33 per month, but in a particular month this can be offset by any money that the pupil has earned *and received* in that month. The chambers cannot roll-over the pupil's earnings, so if a pupil takes in several thousand pounds in received cheques in January but none in February, while the chambers need pay the pupil nothing in January (and can charge a chambers fee on the earnings), it must still pay the £833.33 (or whatever it's monthly guaranteed income is) in February. Crucially, the Inland Revenue has agreed that the first six months of the pupillage award is tax free, and the second half is not.

OTHER FUNDING

The majority of the £3 million that the Inns give out to qualifying barristers goes to those on the **CPE/GDL** and the **BVC**, but between them the Inns do dole out about £150,000 in scholarships to pupils for support during their pupillage year. As far as I can tell, only Gray's Inn awards substantial scholarships (several thousand pounds) to pupils on a merit basis (apply in July before pupillage), and then only a small number of them, the other Inns awarding smaller pupillage-year scholarships on a need/hardship basis.

The professional development loans and essay competitions mentioned above in chapter eight are also open to pupils.

OLPAS AND NON-OLPAS

A little over 50 per cent of pupillages in chambers are offered only through a central applications system, much like UCAS for university applications. This is the OnLine Pupillage Applications Scheme, or **OLPAS**, and is operated through www.pupillages.com. Under OLPAS, the earliest a student may apply for pupillage is in the summer two years before pupillage. For those having no break between their three-year undergraduate degree, BVC, and pupillage, this means the summer at the end of the second year of their degree course. Most chambers, however, will only offer pupillages one year before pupillage, that is, not long before most students start their BVC. The reason for this is that a year earlier still may be too early to evaluate properly the student's legal potential, particularly as those doing a non-law degree will often have done no law at all two and a half years before their pupillage.

OLPAS applications take place in two seasons, summer (with the deadline usually at the start of May and offers made in July) and autumn (with the deadline usually at the end of September and offers made in November). Each application can specify up to 12 chambers. In reality, the summer season is the main one, and most chambers take part only in that season, or at least join the autumn season only if they don't get good applications in the summer one.

Those chambers operating outside OLPAS have their own application forms with their own timetables for applications and interviews. Some of them do this in order to try to cherry pick the best students before the OLPAS offers are made, hoping that such students will take the view that a bird in the hand is worth two in the bush. Others operate timetables that are the same as or later than the OLPAS timetable but just prefer their own application form. It is difficult to generalise, so the potential applicant must investigate as early as possible whether any chambers they may want to apply to are outside OLPAS and, if so, what their timetables are (some application deadlines are as early as January). Non-OLPAS applications are made by sending individual application forms directly to the chambers, and a student may apply to as many of those as he or she wishes. It should be added that chambers outside OLPAS are neither better nor worse than those inside OLPAS, and would-be applicants should look at all possible chambers.

THE PUPILLAGES WEBSITE

All pupillages, whether in OLPAS or not, are listed on www.pupillages.com. This sets out: whether a pupillage is in the OLPAS system, and if so in which season applications should be made; how long the pupillage is, and, if the pupillage is for 12 months, whether it is guaranteed for 12 months or terminable earlier; the amount of the pupillage award; and how far in advance of the pupillage the chambers will take applications.

THE TIMETABLE

The following is the typical timetable although, as mentioned above, in some cases you can do everything a whole year earlier (ie apply two years and five months before pupillage instead of one year and five months beforehand, etc).

The start of May one year and five months before pupillage	OLPAS summer season applications deadline
The end of July one year and two months before pupillage	OLPAS summer season offers
September one year and one month before pupillage	OLPAS autumn season applications
End of October just under a year before pupillage	OLPAS autumn season offers
July before pupillage	Inn Senior Scholarship application deadline
September just before pupillage October	Inn Senior Scholarship interviews Pupillage

Pupillages at the Employed Bar are not advertised through these central systems, and advertising and applications are conducted differently for each organisation. Those interested in such pupillages must therefore contact the organisations directly (and note that some, eg the **GLS**, have very early deadlines: see further chapter one).

APPLICATION FORMS

Your application form or OLPAS form must be a masterpiece: a significant proportion of applicants to a particular chambers, sometimes as high as 90 per cent of several hundred, are weeded out at the application form stage. You are (or should be) trying to convince the chambers that you are independent, a good communicator, careful with words, and good at documentary presentation. There must be no spelling mistakes and no hyperbole. Draft and draft and draft again. Remember that you are up against people doing the same. I must say I find these things nearly impossible myself: it is hard not to speak in clichés ('intellectual challenge' etc), and anything I write here is in danger of becoming one because of readers adopting it for their own use, so I will avoid giving examples and just advise you to strike a realistic tone about what you've already done and why you want to do a certain type of work.

Other general advice is always to answer the question you've been asked (not the one you wished you'd been asked), and not to feel obliged to use the maximum number of words permitted if you don't have anything to say. Succinctness is an important trait in a barrister. The OLPAS form (like the UCAS form) is completed and submitted online. It consists of two sections:

(i) a general section that is seen by all the chambers you have applied to. This mainly concerns your educational history, work experience, and prizes, but also asks why you want to become a barrister (in 150 words or fewer), and which four practice areas (from a list of 17[33]) particularly interest you and why you have chosen these specialisms (again, in 150 words or fewer). These questions are the reason why you really cannot apply through OLPAS to chambers in a wide range of practice areas. For example, if a chambers saw that you were interested in criminal, construction, revenue, and shipping law, then unless your 150-word explanation justifying those choices was extremely good (and I can't imagine what it could say), all of the chambers might conclude that you have not really decided what you want to do and are not serious about their areas of practice, and therefore reject you. There is no problem with having inconsistent specialisms as between your OLPAS form and your applications outside OLPAS, or between the various applications outside OLPAS, since these chambers won't see each others' forms.

(ii) another section in which you can tell each of your chosen chambers why you have chosen them. What you say to one chambers in this section will not be seen by the others, although most chambers will not believe your claims that they are your number one choice because they will assume (rightly or wrongly) that you have said the same thing to all the chambers. You may want to mention what you saw in your **mini-pupillage** at the chambers, or what cases members of that chambers have done, although your personal reasons for liking the chambers will be just as important.

The same comments made in chapter eight in relation to the BVC online form apply here.

---

[33] These are Criminal, Mixed Civil & Crime, Civil, Chancery, Commercial Other than Shipping, Construction, Patent/Intellectual Property, Personal Injury, Professional Negligence, Family, Planning/Environmental, Landlord & Tennant, Revenue, Employment Law, International/EEC, Public Law, Admiralty & Shipping.

A point should perhaps be made about work experience. Remember that you don't have to include all of your experience, and you certainly don't have to give detail about all of your experience. In some cases, your most useful three to six items are probably sufficient; in others you may feel you need a long list but want to provide detail (who you sat with, perhaps, or what you saw) only of a couple of the most impressive or relevant ones. There is nothing wrong with being selective and emphasising (for example) the mini-pupillages in the particular area of practice in which the chambers you are applying to operates and deleting some of the others. This will show the most relevant experience, and also make it look like you really have focused on that area of law. If, however, you have only done a couple of mini-pupillages and they are not in the same field as the chambers you are applying to, then putting them in is better than putting none in, since you want at least to convince the chambers that you know what the Bar is all about.

For your OLPAS form, as well as your CV and non-OLPAS application forms, you will require two referees. At least one of these should be academic, that is, someone at university who has taught you. The other referee should be someone who knows you well through work, mooting, a society or other pastime, university pastoral care, or, alternatively, another academic referee. Obviously it is better if your referees are professors rather than associate lecturers, or qualified barristers rather than your uncle, but ultimately the most important thing is that they know you well enough to provide an honest (and, hopefully, positive) reference.

INTERVIEWS

Each chambers' approach to interviews differs, although you can get some idea about what some of the chambers do at www.chambersandpartners.com/chambersstudent. Many chambers have two rounds of interviews, although some have three. The first will often be a relatively informal chat with one or two members of chambers (although even at this stage they will be looking to eliminate a significant portion of applicants) and will often include a brief discussion of a topical legal issue (sentencing, legal aid, telephone hearings, etc). The second will usually be a more formal exercise in which you will be given some time beforehand to read a particular brief or set of facts and then will be asked to discuss it with the interviewers, who may form a panel of between two and fifteen barristers of various stages of seniority.

The purpose of the interview, from the interviewers' point of view, is to determine whether you will be a good barrister. This comprises handling the legal problem well, but also handling the barracking from the interviewers (just as barristers have to face a barrage of questions and probes from judges) and doing it with some composure and perhaps a little humour. They want to know whether they could work with you, and they will also know that you have prepared for the interview and that they don't have long to take the measure of you. Accordingly, they may throw off-the-wall questions at you (I remember being asked what I would do with a million pounds) as well as the predictable ones.

Prepare yourself as well as you can: read all about the chambers, and read about the cases that members of chambers have been in. Find out about the history of the chambers: Did it formerly practise under a different name? Has it moved premises? Has it merged with another chambers? Does it have a regional outpost? Is it moving into particular practice areas? If you've done a **mini-pupillage**, remind yourself of what you did there and with whom. Revise the legal areas you are likely to be asked about: the interviewers will assume that you have done so and know the law, although will not expect you to know areas you won't have encountered, such as tax, insurance, etc. Think of the answers to all the questions you might be asked. Some are generic (why do you want to be a barrister? why not a solicitor? why a Chancery barrister? why in London?); some more specific (we see from your CV that you spent two years in retail: why did you leave?). Some will relate to current legal topics, and you should read up on them (read *Legal Week*, *The Lawyer*, *Counsel* magazine, and *The Times* law sections). There's always some area of reform of the legal profession that they can ask you about (what makes you think barristers will still be around in 20 years' time? should wigs be abolished? given the rise of employed barristers and solicitor-advocates, what are the essential characteristics of the Bar and barristers?).

You should also note that some of the BVC providers get their students to fill out forms giving details of the interviews at particular chambers. This file of information (if it exists at your **Bar school**) might be useful in giving you a feel for what to expect at the different stages of interview.

Dress smartly in a suit. Arrive promptly (which, in practice, means arriving at chambers early and then, once you've located it, waiting out the extra time in a café nearby). Tell the receptionist who you are and why you are there (and do so nicely—you never know whose views will be sought when a decision is made). When you are told what is going to happen and have been taken into the room (possibly after being given a while in another room with a legal problem to consider), be friendly and shake hands with everyone unless it is impractical to do so (eg a table of 15 people). Address your answers particularly to the person who asked them, but also make eye contact with everyone there from time to time. Be aware that under pressure or when nervous you may feel inclined to withdraw your point or argument, or waver. Try not to do so: everyone is nervous, and the interviewers are aware of that, but you must try to be engaged and amiable. Pause thoughtfully rather than leaping into an answer and then having to rethink or um and ahh. Don't say banal things like 'that's interesting' or 'I see the difficulty' unless you immediately follow up with an answer. In the legal part of the interview (rather than the 'finding out about you' part) the interviewers will probably attack your position whatever it is—don't collapse under the first signs of argument, rather engage with the interviewers' points and argue your case. If it is necessary to alter your view then do so—there is no point in being dogmatic when it is clear that you are wrong—but try not to look like you have capitulated and try to retain something of your position (since as a barrister you are often trying to convince a court of your client's argument, not find out what is the correct view).

Finally, you will be asked whether you have any questions. Don't make something stupid up on the spot, but do try to think of something thoughtful in advance, about the chambers, or its pupillage scheme, or its history of taking on pupils, etc.

HAVING PROBLEMS GETTING PUPILLAGE?

As the statistics show, many students have problems getting a pupillage, and end up taking a job after their BVC finishes while they try to find a pupillage. It then becomes even more difficult because there is no time to research properly, to apply to chambers and to prepare for interviews, and each interview seems that much more important and so that much more stressful. There is no easy answer, except to play the averages: eventually you will have a good interview/fit in well with a chambers/find a chambers which has had only worse applicants than you this year. As if you weren't under enough pressure, you should know that a BVC is valid only for five years before the commencement of pupillage.

However, don't just blame the chambers. If you really want to be a barrister and are barely getting any pupillage interviews then either you are applying to the wrong sets or, more likely, your CV and forms need improving. There are many cases of people who have failed miserably at the first OLPAS application, taken stock over the next year and got as much useful experience as possible, and then been invited for a full complement of interviews and triumphantly secured a pupillage at a great chambers. Many chambers realise that pupillage applications include a lottery element and that your failure to secure pupillage first time round does not make you damaged goods. Indeed, many chambers rightly value perseverance, although they may well ask you in interviews about your former attempts.

The following are some of the ways to increase your chances.

(i)   Perhaps most importantly, get feedback from the chambers that didn't interview you, or those that did but didn't offer you pupillage. Find out what was wrong with your application form or your interview. This will make it much easier to do better next time, and will give you something to focus on constructively.

(ii) Regularly check the 'newsflash' section of the www.pupillages. com website. Some chambers offer extra pupillages, often at very short notice (eg when expected pupils have dropped out).

(iii) Perfect your CV and application. They must be well suited to the particular chambers, so play up your criminal-related experience for criminal sets and play it down a little for other sets. You must make them believe, without saying anything incredible, that this is the area you want to do. Focus on your strengths: if you did well in your degree then focus on that; if you did badly in your degree then deal with that (don't hide the lower second, tackle it head on) and explain that you are a strong **mooter** or that your legal and other experience since university has matured you and sharpened your abilities (if it's true!). Check that you have followed the advice given above about tailoring your OLPAS application to the particular field you are interested in, and not applying (through OLPAS) for chambers in a range of fields.

(iv) Get help. Go to see your Inn student officer, or at least speak to him or her on the phone if you are outside London. Get an Inn **sponsor**, if you don't already have one, and talk to him or her. If you are outside London, contact your local **circuit** and get someone there to give you the local information. Do **judge marshalling** if your Inn provides it. Go to Inn events such as the Cumberland Lodge weekends (even if you have already done all your **qualifying sessions**). Speak to family friends who are barristers, if you are lucky enough to have any. Do as many minis as possible. You need contacts.

(v) Broaden your target. Consider geographical areas you haven't previously applied to, and re-evaluate which areas of law you would be happy to practise in.

(vi) Get useful and impressive experience. You may find you have more time on your hands than you wanted. Use it constructively in the advice clinics, representation units and similar organisations, or earn money while getting good experience in a law-related job (see chapter six). You have to use your initiative and a little bit of drive, but I know of candidates who have gone from getting no interviews to getting interviews from all of the chambers they applied to by spending the intervening year getting useful advice and tightening up their application form. In addition, if you look into it you will probably find that your **Inn** provides lots of opportunities, such as summer and other placements abroad, all of which are great experience and look good on your CV. As well as work opportunities, check out the legal recruitment agencies for jobs as paralegals (assistants in solicitors' firms).

(vii) If you can afford it, you really want to be a barrister and you just can't get a pupillage, think about doing a Master's degree. Normally I would recommend a degree only to people who want to do it for what it is, but it may be the solution for notionally upgrading a bad undergraduate degree result and is not uncommonly taken for this very reason. There are hundreds of LLM programmes in the UK and abroad (see http://www. llm-guide.com/). One of the newest options is the Northumbria LLM in Advanced Legal Practice, which is only available to those with a BVC (or **LPC**) and is (because of its practical leaning) particularly relevant to those wishing to become barristers. (However, those considering this course should still weigh up the reputation, location, facilities, etc, of Northumbria as against the other institutions, and consider whether they would rather do an LLM in a substantive legal area in which they are going to practise rather than in procedural and related topics.)

(viii) Try to get a case comment or short article published in a law journal. If necessary (and this is a cynical ploy) go to a law library, find the journals you have never looked at before and consider submitting a piece to them (they will be less competitive). All you need to do is find out the subject-matter, format, and lengths of pieces for each journal (at least once a year the journal will publish notes for contributors on these matters, and this information will usually also be on a website) and then write about something interesting or topical, perhaps adapted from a dissertation if you ever did one. Then send it in to the relevant editor for consideration. However, it will have to be good to get in, and it can take six months or more for an article to be accepted (acceptance is the key: it can then be put on your CV as 'forthcoming in . . .', even if it is not actually being published for another year).

(ix) Good luck.

11

Life as a Pupil

BECOMING LEARNED

There are always things that you can read up on if you want to get on top of things. The most important will be the law: (re)familiarise yourself with the areas of law that members of your chambers commonly practise, and the recent developments in those areas. You may also want to familiarise yourself with the key rules of procedure and evidence that you will be using (eg civil, criminal, or family). You will have covered these at **Bar school** but it's fair to say there will still be more to learn. Finally, it is worth rereading the Bar **Code of Conduct** and the relevant Schedules to the Code.

LOOKING AND ACTING THE PART

Just as a primary school student doesn't need a full set of precision geometry instruments and a graphical calculator, similarly the pupil barrister doesn't need to start pupillage with eight **court shirts** and three Mont Blanc fountain pens. On the other hand, although it may not be the case that clothes maketh the man, dressing properly and having the right tools is pretty important for convincing both yourself and others that it is only a matter of time before you become a barrister. This is worth some effort because half the battle to getting tenancy is to manage things so that the barristers in your chambers can imagine you doing the job, and not merely being a pupil (even if a very good pupil).

Some people will have been wearing cufflinks in the cradle, but for the rest of us the complex rules of dress (what makes a good suit? which shoes should be worn with which trousers?, etc.) will be somewhat daunting.

The best advice is to pay attention to barristers in your chambers and similar chambers. Style varies from criminal barrister to commercial barrister (for example, family barristers seem to have more leeway in terms of style), so it is difficult to make general comments. Further, although some barristers dress differently, I take the (fairly cowardly) view that the time for dramatic fashion statements comes after pupillage, and probably much later still. If you don't have a strong character then you will find it difficult to carry off distinctive fashion choices, and if you do have a strong character you don't really need distinctive fashion choices. My background is the commercial Bar, and from that standpoint I make the following comments. Barristers wear suits. I had two for my pupillage—navy with light chalk stripes and grey with light chalk stripes—and I alternated them from day to day (to let them 'rest' on the hangers between wears). For men, it is generally the case that price equates to quality, and if you can possibly afford it you should invest in pretty good suits. I'm not talking about tailored Saville Row or Jermyn Street suits, but I'm also not talking about Topman. Spend at least £200 (perhaps in the sales in the shops around law London) and you'll look and feel pretty good, although if you don't have the money, then of course you can get by with a cheaper suit. In case you don't know (and I didn't), a good suit will not have a fashionable cut (such as very high lapels), will probably have vents (slits) in the back of the jacket, the trousers will tighten by means of cloth buckles at the sides rather than a belt, and the jacket will often be lined with a gregarious colour. It's probably worth getting a spare pair of trousers if you can as they are the cheaper part of a suit and wear out far more quickly than jackets.

For women, a trouser suit has the advantage that you can run if necessary, and you can also avoid revealing too much leg to your pupil supervisor or client (as well as avoiding ripping your skirt in car doors, although, apparently, a stapler borrowed from a court office and applied in the toilets to the offending rip, with the staples from the inside to the outside, can save the situation when necessary). Even better is to buy a suit with trousers and a skirt, effectively giving you two suits for the price of one and a bit. For women, I'm told that price does not necessarily equate to quality, and you can get away with a suit from a high street store to start off with. A fairly unusual cut, perhaps in the skirt, will set you apart from the bog-standard suit without making a dramatic statement.

For both men and women, regular dry-cleaning keeps your suit looking new. When the cloth starts to look shiny, bobbly, or shapeless then I'm afraid it's time to pack it off to the charity shop and take a shopping trip.

Court shirts are discussed below. Your normal shirts will generally be plain, with a weave in the fabric being a better way of showing your individuality than a pattern (although you'll soon discover that stripes are common in many chambers). You may not have worn a white shirt since you were in school uniform, but some traditional chambers expect them, particularly for women: as always, the key is to start off with the most conservative clothing and keep an eye on what others in chambers are wearing. Good-quality shirts (although this applies to men's shirts more than to women's) will have bones in their collars (plastic or metallic tabs that can be inserted into the collar points from the inside and removed when washing or ironing), and such shirts will probably set you back over £20. Many shops have two-for-one or three-for-two sales (and such sales seem to me to be so frequent in the TM Lewin chain, in particular, that I would not recommend that you buy shirts in there at any other time).

Shoes are just as important. You can't get away with the school-shoe style that may have sufficed until this point in your life. Shoes now have to look the part. For men, they might be smart, well-made, slip-ons or plainish lace-ups, probably black, almost certainly fairly expensive, but they should last a few years with a bit of polishing (and a timely re-soling or re-heeling at the cobblers when necessary). I got by with two pairs of black shoes, which I also alternated daily. For women, if tights are worn, always carry a spare pair in your handbag, and keep heels low to facilitate the inevitable running with heavy bags or piles of papers across busy roads to court.

As explained above, a barrister has to wear a **court shirt**, **bands**, wig, and gown in court. These can be expensive. A wig, gown, blue bag, and wig case will cost in the region of £800 (the lion's share of that going on the wig), although there are often 'new pupil' deals at the appropriate time of year, as well as a steady availability of unused second-hand wigs and gowns (the unwanted investments of would-be barristers who did not get tenancy: check the notice boards in the **Inns**). Then there are the court shirts, collars, bands, and studs (note that usually you should get collars half an inch larger than the neck size of the court shirts, and that if you lose or forget your studs you can always use your cufflinks for the day to tide you over). How much of this you should buy before pupillage will depend upon your circumstances. If you are rich, confident of getting tenancy, or know that you will need them before the time when you will find out whether you have been offered tenancy, then you will buy them. Ask in your chambers: some barristers like their pupils to wear full court dress when attending court; others think it best that pupils should not wear court dress even in court unless they are **instructed** on a case (ie they are named as one of the barristers and are being paid to appear for the client). I take the latter view, but the important thing is what your pupil supervisor thinks. If you are bound to get a lot of work on your own account in courts other than the magistrates' and county courts then you will need the full court dress anyway. Even then, you could probably avoid buying the bag and wig case until after tenancy is assured (and beyond).

EQUIPPING YOURSELF

As for other kit, a calculator is pretty useful, and a computer (probably a laptop during pupillage) may well be expected: find out from your chambers or a pupil there.

The key books are very expensive. Although useful to own, there is probably no need in pupillage or the first year or two of tenancy to buy your own copy of *The White Book* on court practice, *Chitty on Contracts*, or *Archbold on Criminal Pleadings, Evidence and Practice* (all Sweet & Maxwell). Even as a new tenant you can often get by without by looking online, and borrowing someone else's copy when you need it for court. However, you should be aware that there is a discount of approximately a third available on *The White Book* for those within three years of their call: this is available by means of a form you have to fill in at Wildy & Sons and Hammicks, and, I believe, other legal bookshops (as the reduction is provided by the publisher, Sweet & Maxwell, and not the retailer). You're unlikely to use this during pupillage but bear this in mind in the early years of practice.

I've already spoken about what clothes to wear as a barrister. There are also issues about how you wear them. Keep the shoes polished; button the suit jacket, but only the middle button of three or top button of two; don't wear a rucksack or shoulder bag unless you can't avoid it, rather get a briefcase of some sort (preferably old and battered, like a doctor has, or a small case on wheels, and preferably not one of those eighties-style ones with right-angled corners).

As well as looking the part, you have to act the part: you want the barristers in chambers to have to keep reminding themselves that you're not already a barrister. This means going to all the talks and lectures that other barristers go to in order to be seen (although also to learn what's going on, and, one would hope, because you are interested), even though you don't need the **Continuing Professional Development** (CPD) points that barristers (but not pupils) need to earn each year. Don't look harried or sheepish or as though you don't have a right to be where you are: you have every right. Do take part in conversations or banter with barristers (although there may be rules in this as in everything else).

PUPILLAGE GENERALLY

Pupillage varies dramatically from chambers to chambers and barrister to barrister. Although many chambers have policies on pupillage, and all barristers have to have some training before they become **pupil supervisors**, most of what pupil supervisors know about pupillage comes from what they can remember of their own pupillage ten years before. In addition, the culture of the chambers will affect pupillage: some are very organised and will supervise their pupillages, sorting out when you will go to your next pupil supervisor and all the financial and other details automatically. Others will be a lot more disorganised and will treat each pupillage as if it is the first pupillage they have ever run, with it coming as an apparent surprise when the pupil needs something or needs to go to a new pupil supervisor; and some chambers will treat pupillage as a private matter between the pupil and pupil supervisor and nothing to do with the chambers (which in a sense it is, and certainly in the past it always has been).

YOUR RELATIONSHIP WITH YOUR PUPIL SUPERVISOR

Spare a thought for your pupil supervisor. They are self-employed. They earn money only for the hours they work; they pay rent for their room; and they have agreed to take into their room a pupil for three, six, or twelve months, or if not in their room, at least to supervise you and other pupils and let you follow them around to every conference and every court appearance. Why would they do this? They do it because someone did it for them, because it's good for the chambers to have good juniors (and good juniors start as good pupils), and maybe, just maybe, because they like having pupils around or find them useful. Still, the fact is that pupils can be a burden. It takes time to explain things to pupils, and when pupils are in the room, barristers can't do what they might want to do (make private telephone conversations, play rock music, etc). On the other hand, pupil supervisors have agreed to be pupil supervisors, and they shouldn't do so unless they are prepared to spend the time making the pupillage work for the pupil. There is no excuse for pupil supervisors making their pupils feel useless, awkward, or beholden to them (and I'm afraid there are many stories of this happening).

The upshot of this is that a pupil and pupil supervisor relationship is a slightly odd one. The best way to begin is to raise the ground rules in advance, if your pupil supervisor doesn't do so. In particular, at the beginning you must establish what hours you should work and what lunch break you are to have.

A pupil supervisor will often want the pupil to leave the room so that the pupil supervisor can make a personal telephone call. This could be to family or friends, a bank manager, or a clerk. It may feel awkward, but it is perfectly normal and completely understandable. Moreover, a pupil will often learn many confidential and not so confidential things about the pupil supervisor's family, friends, hobbies, and opinions (they may take swimming lessons on Wednesday evenings, have a weakness for pasties, or something more serious). It is the pupil's duty to keep the confidence and not to share the secrets with the other pupils, or others, however tempting it may be to do so. Be discreet. Apart from anything else, your discretion and ability to keep confidences is one of the important attributes of a good barrister, since just about every case entails your learning private information and seeing confidential communications from your client (including those that the other side of the litigation will never see because they are what is called 'privileged').

Generally a pupil supervisor will not expect or want the pupil to work the same hours as the pupil supervisor does. However, the usual problem is that the pupil supervisor knows more than the pupil about the shape of the coming days (when there are conferences away from chambers, when work is likely to get hectic), and this can make planning lunches and after-work activities difficult. In addition, pupil supervisors often 'do a Columbo', as my fellow pupils and I referred to it. In essence, this involves your pupil supervisor asking you to do or talk about 'just one last thing' as you are about to leave the office for lunch or to go home, and this one last thing invariably proves the undoing of your plans by taking at least half an hour (just as Inspector Columbo's 'just one more thing' question was usually the one that would reveal the murderer in the 1970s and 1990s television series 'Columbo' starring Peter Falk).

A pupil supervisor is not your employer.[34] He or she is unlikely to be able to provide such full facilities for you as his or her own facilities (and this applies whether you are stationed in your pupil supervisor's room or in a pupils' room). It is to be hoped that you will have a desk and chair, but they may not be comfortable. Probably you will be using your laptop rather than a desktop computer. You may or may not have internet access. The latter is relevant as to how easy or enjoyable your life is (and 20 seconds of emailing breaks up three hours of legal drafting like you wouldn't believe), but the desk, chair, and laptop issues are questions of health. Try as best you can to set things up so that you have good posture and good light. I used a wrist-rest for my laptop, and set my laptop on a ring binder so that the keyboard was tilted upwards. I also tried to take walks and look out of the window every now and again.

You may be expected to take turns in making tea and coffee or going on a sandwich run to the local sandwich shop. Some barristers may expect you to do more than take turns, although in reality there is not much you can do unless your menial tasks get out of hand, in which case the largely unrealistic avenue of complaining to your head of chambers becomes available. I have heard of pupils being sent off to help solicitors in setting up a conference room for a talk. This entailed the male pupil un-stacking chairs and the female pupil pushing around a hostess tea trolley. (One of the real tea ladies said to the pupil, as one tea-lady to another, 'cor, your lot make you work late, don't they?'.)

Be aware that your pupil supervisor may not want you to eat smelly sandwiches (or any sandwiches) in her or his room, and that even if

---

[34] Nor is your chambers. It was decided by the Court of Appeal in the case of *Edmunds v Lawson* [2000] QB 501 that, although pupils do have a contract with their chambers, they are not apprentices or employees within the meaning of the minimum wage legislation.

you eat them out of the room you may want to have some mints handy to make yourself a better roommate. In fact, if you have the time, I would advise you to try to have lunch with other pupils in or outside your chambers (you will know some from Bar School and university) and to take advantage of the Inn lawns in summer. I have also heard of a pupil being told by her pupil supervisor's room-mate that he was allergic to her perfume.

CHAMBERS TEA

Some chambers conduct a tea ritual at a certain hour every afternoon. All barristers not otherwise engaged are expected to attend, although often only the three or four most senior people in the room will conduct conversation, to which everyone else will listen (while drinking tea). I have been witness to a chambers tea during a mini-pupillage. Other than by means of a time machine or a bad dream, this is something you are likely to witness only in very traditional Chancery sets. (This should not be confused with the entirely sensible, if also sometimes stressful for pupils, gathering for tea in some chambers where everyone just chats to each other.)

SITTING IN COURT

You should bow when a judge comes in or leaves, just as the barristers do. Act professionally, not fiddling or looking bored. Before the first court appearance, establish what you are expected to do in court, that is, whether you should pass notes to your pupil supervisor, or take a full note of what happens, or just sit and listen. This will depend upon the type of hearing but also on the particular barrister. Certainly take a note of any judgment or order granted—your pupil supervisor will probably do the same but often it is difficult to keep up with the judge and you are more likely to have everything down between the two of you than if only one took a note.

Probably you will sit behind your pupil supervisor, often with the **instructing solicitor**, although sometimes even further back (your pupil supervisor should indicate where you are to sit the first few times you are in court). If you've been involved in the case, the situation may arise when you think there is an important factual point or legal argument that your pupil supervisor is not making and should make. If you are sure it will help, then pass a note to your pupil supervisor, although this is a high-risk strategy: many pupil supervisors will not want to be interrupted in mid-flow, your point may not in fact be a good one or may be one the pupil supervisor has already thought of, and in any case some pupil supervisors will never listen to you.

SITTING IN A CONFERENCE

If anything, sitting in a conference is more of a minefield for the pupil than sitting in court. Before the first conference with solicitors or clients, you need to establish whether you are permitted to speak or whether you should remain silent—this will depend upon your pupil supervisor, how much you know about the case, and how far along in pupillage you are. The atmosphere in the conference may be relaxed, but you should still think very carefully before speaking, unless your pupil supervisor has told you that he or she doesn't mind. Take notes of important things, and try not to fall asleep. It is also important to resist the temptation to rush for the biscuits and the sandwich lunch when it arrives; your boredom will naturally lead both to hunger and to incredulity at how the other people in the conference are so nonchalantly pretending to be interested in what is being said and not in the food.

ADVOCACY AND OTHER EXERCISES

During pupillage you will have advocacy exercises, both compulsory ones in your Inn and, quite possibly, exercises laid on by your chambers. Having done the BVC you'll know what to do. With the Inn exercises, really work on learning as much as you can—they are genuinely useful and are often in front of real judges. The ones in chambers are obviously more tense, and the most important thing is to show that you do not make any mistake twice: pay close attention to any negative feedback after the first exercise and make sure that you take it on board next time (even if you then make another entirely different mistake). Many chambers follow the approach agreed by the

Inns of providing no positive feedback and restricting themselves to one or two points of negative feedback (ie points for improvement). This is supposed to be constructive, giving you one thing to focus on for next time, but invariably it makes you feel like you are completely incompetent.

SOCIALISING WITH YOUR CHAMBERS

Some chambers regularly gather inside or outside chambers for drinks, and sometimes pupils are invited along to drink with the clerks. Apart from the fact that socialising is actually fun (lest we forget), getting to know people in your chambers is generally an excellent idea for all sorts of obvious reasons. There are pitfalls to watch out for, however. First, while a pupil, it is best to avoid spending more time with the clerks than with barristers, as the barristers (who decide whether you get tenancy) may take against you or may not to be able to imagine you as a barrister. Second, don't make a fool of yourself by getting drunk at chambers events (drinks parties etc). Some chambers don't even invite their pupils to their chambers Christmas or other parties. Third, no sex with anyone in chambers during pupillage. Whether you have a secret liaison or not, and whether the whole thing works out or not, this can cause unforeseeable problems for your tenancy decision. Fourth, as a pupil you are in limbo. It is often said that a pupillage is a year-long interview, and all the barristers are the interview panel. While people will generally be friendly to you, in most chambers pupils come and go every year, and after a while barristers and others start to think that it is not worth the effort properly getting to know someone who may not be in chambers more than a year (which is the reason why your older lecturers at university didn't bother to learn your name). After you get tenancy you may notice barristers miraculously becoming more affable, knowing your name, and asking about you, whereas before tenancy they didn't even seem to know whether you were a pupil or a burglar. Nevertheless, you have to do your best to be friendly to them, and it is surprising how often it will be met not with a blank stare but with a bit of banter. This may help when it comes to 'The Decision' and beyond.

DEALING WITH MINI-PUPILS

Be nice: you used to be them and they want to be you.

DEALING WITH SOLICITORS

If you can naturally strike up a rapport with your pupil supervisor's instructing solicitors then that is great: when they phone chambers in a year's time looking for a junior barrister they may remember your name. However, never try to overshadow your pupil supervisor; you are there in a support role at most.

DEALING WITH OTHER PUPILS

How you handle your relationship with the other pupils is very important. As well as being your competitors, they are your natural allies and the best people to assuage your concerns when you think you've screwed something up ('oh yes, he said the same thing to me when he saw my draft defence in January'). The gossip and exchange of information between pupils can also be invaluable, and they are the only people who really understand how you feel. As long as the situation permits (ie it will be difficult if there are two pupils and one tenancy place, or six pupils going for two tenancies), you should try to get on and to spend time together. Go for a drink after work or for lunch as often as possible—you'll be glad you did when you come to the few months before The Decision. Remember also that if you are aggressive competitors you'll have problems if you and other pupils do get tenancy—they will be your peer group and your most likely friends. Having said all of the above, I should add that you should be prudent and discreet: don't gush your feelings and your own and your pupil supervisors' secrets to other pupils, because they may not be nice enough to keep them to themselves. There is one blanket rule that applies in all situations: never backstab or manipulate or practise gamesmanship, and always be honest. Quite apart from the morality of the thing, a reputation for dishonesty, even if unfairly exaggerated, is the kiss of death for a barrister's career.

TAKING HOLIDAYS

Most chambers will be fairly flexible about your taking holidays, but you should try to coordinate them with those of your pupil supervisors so as to make things easier for your chambers. Don't forego all holidays, but don't be over-indulgent.

FORMS AND ADMIN

At the start of pupillage you must register your pupillage with the Records Department of the **Bar Council** (handling it on behalf of the **Bar Standards Board**), and every time you change pupil supervisor or chambers you must fill in and send off the relevant form notifying the Bar Council of your change in pupillage circumstances (yes, a mere rotation to a new pupil supervisor counts as a change in pupillage circumstances). You should also register your pupillage with the Advocacy or other relevant department of your Inn so that they can notify you of the compulsory courses that you must do during your pupillage (see later in this chapter).

> Remember to register your pupillage with the Bar Council and your Inn upon commencement.

After six months you must complete and post to the Bar Council (again, for the **BSB**) the relevant form applying for a certificate of completion of the non-practising six months of pupillage. This form needs to be signed by the person who was your pupil supervisor at the end of the first six.

After the second six you must submit to the Bar Council the relevant form applying for a certificate of completion of the practising six months of pupillage.

Another thing you're supposed to do is register with the Information Commission, a governmental organisation that records all the people and companies that store information on other people and companies, as an 'information controller' (www.ico.gov.uk) and set up a direct debit to pay them their annual fee (of about £35 at the time of going to press). Email them or phone them up and tell them you are a barrister and they will send you a form completed according to the barrister template, saving you most of the work. This may appear to be something of a scam (since no one is going to check with the Information Commission what your fairly generic list contains), but it is the law. While on pupillage you are covered by your pupil supervisor's **professional indemnity insurance**, but afterwards you need to have your own insurance policy (provided by the Bar Mutual Indemnity Insurance Fund). Having insurance is a requirement of the **Code of Conduct** but, more than that, is of crucial importance to cover you in case of mishap—you do not want to lose your house (if you manage to get one) if you are ever negligent and sued for it. Usually your insurance will be organised through your chambers, and your insurance premium will depend upon how much cover you want (ie the maximum amount the insurance company would pay out if you were sued), but your premium is likely to be between £100 and £200 per year at the beginning of your career.

Key Admin Dates	
Start of non-practising six	Register pupillage and pupil supervisor with the Bar Council.
	Sort out your **call** with your Inn if you haven't done so already (this applies only to those not covered by the proposed new **deferred call** regime).
Every change of pupil supervisor	Register change of circumstances with the Bar Council.
Completion of non-practising six	Apply to the Bar Council for certificate of completion of non-practising six.
Completion of practising six	Apply to the Bar Council for certificate of completion of pupillage.
	Arrange **professional indemnity insurance** through your chambers. Sort out your call with your Inn (if you are subject to the proposed new deferred call regime).
Accepting tenancy offer	Register with the Information Commission as an Information Controller.

YOUR PUPILLAGE CHECKLIST AND RECORDS OF WORK DONE AND THINGS SEEN

During your pupillage you are required to complete the Bar Standards Board's **pupillage checklist**. This is a long list of things (conferences, types of application and hearing, types of documents) that you tick when you have witnessed/done them. Your relevant pupil supervisor will then sign the list to confirm your ticks. The checklist itself contains spaces for writing in the relevant experience, but I would advise you to download an electronic copy of the checklist and add to it as you go along on your computer. I would also advise you to keep a better record than merely the checklist, and record what work you did for whom on what case and when. You can later more easily fill in your pupillage checklist from this more detailed record, and you may need the information for other purposes (reminding yourself what you did for a pupil supervisor and when, etc). You needn't worry when you can't fill all the boxes on the pupillage checklist—that is inevitable and won't stop the Bar Standards Board approving the checklist and granting you your practising certificate.

COMPULSORY COURSES

There are two courses that must be completed during the pupillage training period; otherwise, a pupil (even if he or she has completed a pupillage) will not be granted a final practising certificate and will not be able to practise as a barrister. At the moment, the compulsory courses are the following:

• an advocacy training course (during the **first six**);
• an 'advice to counsel' course;

A third course in forensic accountancy must be done either during pupillage or the first three years of practice.

Your Inn will notify you automatically of the courses, providing you have registered your pupillage with it.

YOUR FINANCES

Self-employed barristers act as an independently accountable unit, like a one-man company. By becoming a barrister, where formerly you were probably only ever an employee, you take on the responsibility to prepare your own tax returns and to account for VAT and various other financial obligations, although such an arrangement is more flexible than that for employees and allows for savings that an employee would not be able to make. Disclaimers are always important, but this one doubly so: the following is meant merely as an introduction to some of the financial issues barristers and pupils face.

Unless you are an expert, you simply must get your own accountant, and early, preferably during pupillage. Many of the accountancy firms that deal with barristers will give you their services free for the first year or so. Get a recommendation from somebody. Other than an accountant, the best and, so far as I know, only good introduction to this important subject is the Bar Council's *Taxation and Retirement Benefits Handbook,* the fourth (and currently latest) edition of which was published in 2002. The *Handbook* is available for free from the Bar Council's website, and see also the HM Revenue's *Notes on Self-Employment* and *Help Sheet IR222.*

It was mentioned earlier that you should keep receipts for purchases for seven years prior to commencement of practice (the start of your **second six**). You must continue to do so beyond commencement and throughout your practice. You can then make deductions for capital purchases (enduring items such as your wig, gown, computer, and law books) and revenue items (other expenses such as courses, lectures, stationery, chambers' rent, mobile phone bills, **professional indemnity insurance** premiums, any law magazine or professional association subscription costs, the cost of travel to court or solicitors' offices from chambers (but not the cost of travel from home to chambers), the cost of subsistence (eg sandwiches) when away from chambers and home on business (but not the cost of subsistence when living at home and working in chambers), bank charges, etc). You can also claim the VAT back (see below).

Taking into account chambers' expenses and taxes, at least a third and generally more like half of what you earn (comprising income tax and the chambers fee of 10 to 15 per cent) is not yours to keep. The ideal solution is to open a separate bank account and to pay the VAT and half of the rest of your earnings (including half of your second six pupillage award) into it as you receive them, so that when your chambers and tax and VAT bills come you will have the money ready. At the end of the tax year you can then take whatever is left and put it back into your everyday bank accounts. The benefits of having a separate account, rather than keeping it in your current account, are, first, that you won't accidentally spend it, and second, that if you take it out of your current account and put it into a savings account it will earn more interest (which you get to keep). (If you have an offset mortgage then you may well want an account linked to that, but that is another story.) Of course, in their early years many barristers will not be able to live on only half of their income after VAT, and so will not be able to put so much aside, but this will make it much more difficult to deal with income tax bills in particular (see below).

Key Financial Dates:

- *Commencement of practising six months*: register as self-employed (although you may want to register at the commencement of your first six).
- *Acceptance of tenancy offer*: consider registering for VAT.
- *January of your first year of tenancy*: the deadline for your first income tax return (although this may depend upon the dates of your pupillage), and also your first half of your payment on account for the following year's tax bill.

National Insurance Class 2 Contributions

After your **first six** months of pupillage, you must register with HM Revenue & Customs as self-employed and set up a direct debit to pay your Class 2 National Insurance contributions. Don't worry, they are small: about £2 per week. If you do not register within three months you will be liable to pay a fine of £100. Once you are registered as self-employed, you will be required to file annual self-assessment tax returns so that HM Revenue and Customs can work out how much income tax and Class 4 National Insurance contributions you have to pay: it is only people in employment who have their tax taken out of their pay under the PAYE (pay as you earn) scheme.

Income Tax

The tax year (or 'fiscal year') runs from 6 April to the following 5 April. In January a self-employed person must pay their income tax bill for the fiscal year that ended in the previous April. However, the tax-payer is also obliged to make payments to the Inland Revenue on account of the next tax bill, estimated from the previous year's bill. Accordingly, if the first relevant fiscal year of a barrister's practice runs from 6 April 2011 to 5 April 2012 and leads to an income tax bill of £20,000, the barrister will pay a £20,000 tax bill for the 2011/2012 tax year in January 2013 and at that same time will also have to make a payment on account of the 2012/2013 tax bill of £10,000, with another £10,000 payment on account due in July 2013. This first January is therefore the hardest. Even if the barrister then makes a bit more in the year from 6 April 2012 to 5 April 2013, say enough to lead to a tax bill of £24,000, then in January 2014 he will only have to pay £4,000 for his 2012/2013 tax bill (because he's already paid £20,000 on account) as well as £12,000 on account for the next bill (with another £12,000 payment on account due in July 2014). If the barrister makes less money in 2012/2013 than 2011/2012 then he will get a refund in January 2014, and his payments on account for January and July 2014 will be less than £10,000 each.

The usual position is that the first six months of any pupillage award is tax free, and the second six months of the award counts as taxable income. The tax year runs from April to March. This means that if you did a 12-month pupillage from October 2010 to September 2011, you may not have to pay any income tax for the fiscal year from 6 April 2010 to 5 April 2011 because your **first six** from October 2010 to April 2011 is not taxable and so you have not actually made any taxable income in the relevant fiscal year (although if your **second six** started much before 6 April then you may have received pupillage award or other income in the 2010/2011 fiscal year and so will have to do a tax return for that year). You will have to pay tax for the next fiscal year, from 6 April 2011 to 5 April 2012, which will include the pupillage award for your second six from April 2011 to September 2011, as well as your earnings as a barrister from that period and the following six months. The tax bill for this year, due in January 2013 along with a payment on account of the following year (as discussed in the previous paragraph) will come as a huge sting if you are unprepared, although in practice most pupils will not have sufficient money to keep aside any of their pupillage award to cover the tax bill to come (I know I certainly couldn't) and so this all forms part of the cash-flow difficulties of early practice. There are other intricacies, for example, you may be able to set your accounting period dates such that you can defer quite a lot of your tax until later years, and so you must do your own investigations or, even better, get yourself an accountant as soon as possible after your commencement of practice.

Value Added Tax (VAT)

At some point after your first six months you may want to become VAT-registered with HM Revenue & Customs. Once you are registered, you (ie your clerk or whoever prepares your **fee notes**) must charge VAT on your services (ie add 17.5 per cent to your bill to the solicitors) and must pay this money over to HM Revenue & Customs every quarter, effectively acting as a tax collector. In return for doing this, there are two major benefits:

(i)   you earn interest on the VAT you have charged (which is really the government's money and which you wouldn't have unless you were VAT registered) from the time when it is paid to you to the time when you have to pay it to the tax man (every quarter);

(ii) although you must pay VAT on goods and services you buy from shops and others whether you are VAT registered or not (providing your suppliers themselves are VAT registered), if you are registered you are entitled to 'claim the VAT back'. This basically means that when calculating the amount of VAT that you have charged your clients and must pay to HM Revenue & Customs, you are allowed to deduct (and therefore keep) an amount equal to the amount of money you have paid in VAT on business-related expenses

(such as two suits per year, taxis, stationery, etc, although note that there is no VAT charged or reclaimable on books, newspapers, food or public transport). Note also that, at present, you can claim back VAT for all relevant goods purchased in the three years prior to registration for VAT, and all services in the six years prior to registration for VAT. In particular, you should be able to get back the VAT on your robes, wig, and computer. This can provide a helpful few hundred pounds in those early months when cash flow is a problem, and registering as soon as you qualify means that your prior three years will catch the maximum number of expenses. The explanation for the VAT system is that the government takes in VAT on every sale to an end user, but if you can show that you are using the item or service for which you have paid for the purposes of producing your own services, you are not the end user, but rather are (in a way) modifying what you bought and selling it on, and so you are allowed to claim back the VAT you paid but must pay on to the government the VAT you take in at the next stage.

It is not compulsory to register for VAT unless you earn over £61,000 per year, but many barristers choose to do so voluntarily on commencement of **tenancy** because their chambers prefers to account that way, because they expect to earn £61,000 per year sooner or later, or in order to claim the VAT back on the things that they buy. (Whether you are registered or not you will pay VAT on everything you buy from other VAT-registered companies and people such as shops and taxi drivers, but if you are not VAT registered you do not need to charge VAT in your bills to your clients.) Registering for VAT is unlikely to deter solicitors from instructing you even though it adds 17.5 per cent to their bill, as they can claim that VAT back, offsetting it against the VAT that they charged the lay client.

When you register, you can choose the dates from which your relevant VAT quarters run. If your chambers does things (such as charging your rent or sorting your invoices) on a quarterly basis you may want your VAT quarters to coincide with your chambers' quarters.

THE TENANCY DECISION

Your chambers should notify you as to when the tenancy decision will be made. Many chambers require their pupils to apply formally for tenancy, and many others merely assume that unless they have been told otherwise their pupils are interested in tenancy.

Generally, the tenancy decision consists of a meeting of the chambers (to which you are not invited) in which everyone has their say, although often there is a pupillage committee that has been paying closer attention to your performance so far and therefore gives a recommendation. There's nothing you can do but wait. Some pupils wait together, for near-unbearable solidarity. Others meet their friends and wait by the phone. Still others sit alone checking for third sixes on the web (I was in this category, although I have endured the painful wait with friends during their decisions).

If successful, you must register your tenancy with the Advocacy or other relevant department of your Inn so that they can notify you of **CPD** courses that you have do during your first three years as a tenant (as part of the 'New Practitioners' Programme').

12

Work as a Pupil

PAPERS

Often you will be working on your pupil supervisor's copy of the papers in a particular case, rather than having your own copy. If you are using their copy, it is generally best never to take them home to work on, both because if you lost them it would be very embarrassing for you and your pupil supervisor, and because your pupil supervisor may also want to work on the papers that evening or weekend (something might just come up). Photocopy the relevant bits or at least check with your pupil supervisor if you do have to take papers home.

RESEARCH

It is a shock to the system to leave Bar school and no longer have free access to the electronic materials available through the Athens website.[35] In some areas of law it is simply impossible to do the job without access to at least one online law database. Find out whether your chambers has an organisational subscription to any of the databases, or whether your pupil supervisor has a subscription for which you can borrow the password while working for him or her. If you are near an Inn library or university library you can access the databases there for free. Buying your own access is a last resort, and a pupil really can't be expected to have to do this.

[35] Athens is a central website that provides university students with access to all the electronic resources (databases etc) to which their particular university has subscribed (see http://www.athens. ac.uk).

Even if you don't have access to the paid databases, there is always Bailii (the British and Irish Legal Information Institute), which is a website holding most new and some old judgments.[36] Be aware that the Civil Procedure Rules and related materials are available online (for free) at http://www.dca.gov.uk/procedurerules.htm, although of course this does not include the helpful commentaries and case references that can be found in *The White Book* (mentioned above) and *The Green Book, Civil Court Practice* (LexisNexis, annual), and in *Blackstone's Civil Practice* (Oxford University Press, annual).

As one might expect, a large proportion of legal research is still done in books. The first port of call will be the pupil supervisor's bookshelf and chambers library (if it has one). The next port of call for the London pupil will be the Inn library closest to chambers. If these don't have what you want, you may have to try the British Library (near King's Cross in London: journals have to be ordered two days in advance, but books take one hour to come up from the catacombs), the Institute of Advanced Legal Studies (the best legal collection held on accessible shelves in the country, also known as the IALS, and found on Russell Square in London), or one of the university libraries. All but your chambers and Inn libraries are likely to be difficult to join and access (although some chambers have corporate membership of the IALS). Of course, the very last resort for obtaining a book is to buy it. Don't do it if you can avoid it (but if you do, keep the receipt for tax and VAT purposes).

Splash out on photocopy cards. In most libraries they save you money when compared with paying as you go with coins, plus you can ask for a receipt for your purchase which you can store away for the time you have to prepare your income tax return. In addition, it is inevitable that you won't have any coins when you most need them, whereas photocopy cards can't be spent on buses or beer.

You will get to know the key 'bibles' in your area of law very quickly, if you don't know them already: *Chitty on Contracts* and *Archbold on Criminal Pleading, Evidence and Practice* (mentioned above) are indispensable in their respective fields. However, you will also get to know the key works on various more precise areas (such as *McGee on Injunctions*). Search the library catalogue, or look in Lincoln's Inn Library's helpful index of textbooks arranged by subject.

---

[36] http://www.baili.org.

PREPARING BUNDLES

For a case to used in court, the copy produced or the citation to the case must be taken from the report that is the highest possible in the following list: 1) the *Official Law Reports* (AC: Appeal Cases, KB/QB: King's Bench, Queen's Bench, Ch: Chancery); 2) the *Weekly Law Reports* (WLR); 3) *The All England Law Reports* or *Lloyd's Law Reports*; 4) any other law report, or full transcript if unreported; 5) a summary, such as in *Current Law*.

If you (or your pupil supervisor) are producing a case from the *Official Law Reports* for a court bundle, then, if at all possible, don't waste time and money photocopying from the paper reports, instead print it off from JUSTIS, if you have access to it. (The web version, at least, allows you to print off exact copies of the paper reports.)

WRITTEN WORK

For many pupils, particularly those in commercial or Chancery chambers, the majority of their days will be spent doing written work. Such work may range from advices and pleadings to skeleton arguments and draft orders.

Computers can be great savers of time. It is worth spending some time creating document templates in your word-processing program (probably Microsoft Word) with all the correct formatting and styles set up for the major documents you use. More than once I've had to draw up an order with a back-sheet (the formal sheet at the back of a document with the parties' names etc) in minutes and been saved by my Word template.

How to do good written work is way beyond the scope of this book, but here are a few pointers: don't rely too heavily on the precedents in the books (*Atkin's Court Forms*, your drafting manual from Bar school, etc) because they are not without flaws; be very careful in your terminology (a judge grants an order, but allows an appeal and enters judgment; you can admit an allegation but aver one of your own); in advices, tread a line between being non-committal and categorical— for advice to be useful you have to advise rather than just explaining how difficult everything is, but on the other hand, law is almost never something so simple that you can state it without any qualification;

when you think your piece of work is finished and ready to show to your pupil supervisor, do yourself a favour and have a very critical extra read through and final search on the legal database for the pertinent case (etc) before clicking on 'send'.

WORK ON YOUR OWN ACCOUNT

During the non-practising six months of pupillage, a pupil is not entitled to supply legal services or to exercise rights of audience. The only paid work he or she is entitled to do as a barrister is a **noting brief**, which is where a pupil gets paid to attend court and take notes on what occurs (often because the client is interested in the proceedings, but does not actually need to attend personally or to be represented at them). In most chambers, noting briefs are rare.

During the practising six months of pupillage, with the permission of his or her head of chambers or pupil supervisor (under whose **professional indemnity insurance** cover the pupil is acting), a pupil may do everything that a barrister may do. In criminal and common law sets, the second six pupil will probably be up and running their own cases very early on, whereas a commercial or Chancery pupil will probably not get many of their own cases nor appear in court much until he or she becomes a tenant.

Some of the paid work a pupil does may not be on instructions by a solicitor: sometimes a barrister will pay a pupil to do some research or other work for the barrister, and in that case the pupil is said to be '**devilling**' for the barrister (and to be the barrister's devil). When devilling, the client is the barrister: it is the barrister who is invoiced by the pupil (ie the pupil's **clerk**), and the solicitors have no relationship with the pupil.

Often a pupillage award is paid on terms that it is in lieu of payment for any individual item of work, but where this is not the case a barrister must pay a pupil for any work done for him or her 'which because of its value to him warrants payment' (Bar *Code of Conduct*).

It is worth setting up a system for recording the (paid) work you have done. I found the best way to do this to be a workbook in Microsoft Excel, with one worksheet recording the details of each case, another recording the hours done on each case, and another recording my expenses and working out my VAT return.

STANDING UP IN COURT

That first walk down to court on your own brief really makes you feel like you've arrived as a barrister. As Henry Cecil observes in *Brothers in Law* (London, Michael Joseph, 1955) at p 17:

> When you go in to court for the first time you'll have a nice white wig and a little theoretical knowledge, but, for the rest, you'll be supported by the love of your parents and the admiration of your girlfriends.

Do strut—you've earned it—but make sure you're prepared. I don't mean with the actual case, or with the rules of procedure, although of course they are important: I mean to ask clerks or others before you go about the key things you will otherwise worry about, such as what to wear (is the hearing robed or can you just wear a suit?), where to sit, the way things will go, and, crucially, how to address the judge (is he or she Sir/Madam, Your Honour, a Registrar, or My Lord/My Lady?)[37]. You should always be nice to court officials such as **ushers**. Problems and delays are rarely their fault, and they can often be important to your case. An unusual example of this arose before my second court appearance. I was sitting outside court talking to the other barristers about what we had to sort out in our imminent case management hearing (since, as usual, the instructions from our solicitors were incomplete) when a court official walked over and said that the court had received a telephone call to say that the barrister for a further party in our case would be 15 minutes late. I asked the guy if he would tell the judge. He paused for a minute, and said in a baritone voice reminiscent of the voice that came down to Moses on Mount Sinai (at least as presented in the film 'The Ten Commandments'), '*I AM the judge*'.

The basic rules of court-work:
1) Always carefully read all your papers: don't assume that the familiar-looking ones that are usually unimportant are in fact unimportant.
2) Prepare for every point that might come up, not just the ones you want or expect to come up.
3) Turn up an hour before each hearing if you can.

---

[37] For the correct forms of address, see http://www.judiciary.gov.uk/about_judiciary/forms_of_address/index.htm.

4) Treat everyone with respect, especially those who you are finding irritating or incompetent (the **litigant-in-person**, the stupid opponent, the slow solicitor, the unhelpful court official). You are no more important than them.
5) Don't overlook obvious and basic points when presenting your case. They may not be as obvious as you think, at least to the judge.

You will probably be fairly nervous in your first appearance in court, which will usually be a very small matter (a criminal mention or a civil case management application) but will still cause you to do a week's worth of preparation. It is important to arrive in court early so that you have time to work out where things are and what you have to do. Invariably, however, you will arrive in court far too early, and will then pace around for three hours trying to look like a barrister and scrutinising others to discern what it is that (as far as you are concerned) makes you look different. You will worry that your wig and gown are not on straight (in fact they are, which is what marks you out as inexperienced). You will forget to ask for things for which your solicitors told you to ask (remember to prepare what your position is on costs, although if you lose, it generally won't matter), and you will fail to get a proper note of what the judge ordered. In my first appearance I was in the High Court opposing the other side's application to extend the time for service of their defence by two weeks. I strenuously opposed, as my solicitors instructed me to do (although fortunately I told them we would probably lose), arguing that two weeks was too long and in fact they should have no extension. The judge gave them three weeks.

Really, it's not that difficult. Most 'barristerliness' comes from a sort of method acting—when you put yourself in the position of barrister and find yourself in court or in a conference you will adopt the role and voice of a barrister if only to satisfy the expectations of those around you. This role-play becomes habit and, before you know it, you are not pretending any more.

Generally, judges and barristers will be nice to you, but sometimes it can be worth posturing. In his first court appearance, my friend was met with an opponent who calculated the interest due on a particular judgment and then said 'my learned friend may want to verify that' and passed the calculator to my friend. My friend took the calculator, pushed some buttons determinedly (but nevertheless at random), and made sure to press the clear key before handing it back to his opponent with a flourish and an 'I am satisfied, Your Honour'.

13

Alternative Careers

If you've given up on the Bar then you must have failed to get pupillage, had your fill of **third sixes** or squatting, or simply decided you don't want to be a self-employed or employed barrister. If so, then, strictly speaking, you've stepped outside the scope of this book. If you've completed pupillage, then you are a qualified barrister, just without a chambers. Even if you haven't completed pupillage, you still have the BVC and probably some further experience. This experience is valuable both inside and outside the law.

As far as law-related careers go, an obvious alternative is to become a solicitor. Solicitors' firms will be very interested in you, particularly the medium-sized and larger firms with litigation departments, and particularly if you have some civil law experience. You can either cross-qualify as a solicitor, which doesn't take too long (you do the Qualified Lawyers Transfer Test), or, as more often happens, work in the solicitors' firm as an employed barrister and then consider cross-qualifying later. As well as the rest of the Employed Bar (ie other than solicitors' firms), there are various other law-related jobs (see http://www.lawcareers.net/Barristers/AlternativeCareers/and http://www.thelawyer.com/students/guide/alternative_careers.html).

Of course, the other option is a non-law-related job. Most jobs in service or other sectors (accountancy, management, finance, marketing, media, publishing, retail, etc) will welcome your skills and qualifications, and you have to fancy your chances against your competitor who just studied history for three years and has no other qualifications or experience! You could write a book: At least in Victorian times, nearly 20 per cent of novelists (including Thackeray and Wilkie

Collins) were failed barristers.[38] And there's always politics: according to official figures, over five per cent of MPs (including Tony Blair) come from the less than 0.001 per cent of the English and Welsh population who are barristers.[39]

[38] John Sutherland, *Victorian Fiction: Writers, Publishers, Readers* (London, 1995), 162.

[39] http://www.parliament.uk/commons/lib/research/notes/snsg-01528.pdf. A higher percentage still are qualified solicitors, teachers, and doctors, but then there are a lot more solicitors, teachers, and doctors in England and Wales than there are barristers.

14

Transferring to the Bar After Practising Abroad or as a Solicitor

There is no nationality requirement for barristers in England and Wales, so anybody (a Ghanaian accountant, Russian librarian, English plumber, etc) who satisfies all of the requirements above (a law degree or **CPE**, a **BVC**, a **pupillage**, etc) may become a barrister. However, for solicitors from England and Wales, and for many lawyers who qualified and practised in foreign countries, there is a shorter route to becoming a barrister than the one described above, and it is the shorter route that is explained in this chapter.

THE SHORTER PROCESS FOR SOME TRANSFERRING LAWYERS

Those for whom there is a special transfer process, that is, solicitors, foreign lawyers, and distinguished English and Welsh legal academics, must gain the approval of the Qualifications Committee of the **Bar Standards Board** and join one of the **Inns of Court**.[40] Once that approval is granted, the relevant candidate will be exempt from the usual requirements of a **qualifying law degree** or **CPE/GDL** and the **BVC**. Instead, such lawyers will have to do some or all of the Bar Standards Board's **aptitude test**, a set of oral and written exams on the law and practice of England and Wales (of which more below). Many

---

[40] See further http://www.barstandardsboard.org.uk.

	Step one: Apply to the Bar Standards Board	Step two: Join an Inn	Step three: The Bar Standards tude test	Step four: Pupillage
Northern Irish Barrister of three years' experience	Yes	Yes	No	Not if one has already been completed in Northern Ireland
Scottish advocate	Yes	Yes some of it	Possibly	Possibly some
Irish barrister of three years' experience	Yes	Yes	No	No
European lawyer (meaning a European national with rights of audience in a European country)[41]	Yes	Yes	Yes	No (although a voluntary period is recommended)
Common law lawyer[42] *or Hong Kong lawyer of three years' experience (and subject to visa requirements)*	Yes	Yes	Usually some or all	Usually some
Solicitors in England and Wales and	Yes	Yes	Sections 4 and 5	Probably some
Solicitor-advocates in England and Wales and Northern Ireland	Yes	Yes	No	Not if the transferor has higher rights of audience in both civil and criminal. Some will be required if the transferor has higher rights of audience in only one of the two.
Distinguished legal academic in England and Wales of distinction	Yes	Yes	No	Possibly some

[41] Including Northern Irish and Irish barristers of with under three years' experience.
[42] At present there is no official Bar Council list of the countries which count as being common law countries. A likely list includes the following, although any candidate who is unsure should check with the Bar Council: Australia, Canada, Fiji, India, Ireland, Malawi, Malaysia, New Zealand, Singapore, South Africa, Thailand, the US (with the likely exception of Louisiana).

such lawyers will also be granted an exemption by the Bar Standards Board from part or all of the usual requirement of a year's **pupillage**. The table below shows the requirements for transfer to the Bar for the various different types of transferring lawyer. Those not included in the table (such as **legal executives** in England and Wales, legal practitioners in civil law jurisdictions outside Europe, and foreign legal academics) must follow the ordinary rules set out elsewhere in this book (ie do a law degree, BVC, pupillage, etc). (It should be noted, however, that the Bar Standards Board is in the process of simplifying these rules when it replaces its old Consolidated Regulations with new Training Regulations, so potential applicants should check the www.legaleducation. org.uk website for the latest information.)

Step One: the Application to the Bar Standards Board

The first step is to apply to the Bar Standards Board. All the relevant forms and guidance notes are available on the website www.barstandardsboard.org.uk, or you can get further information from the Secretary of the Qualifications Committee at the Bar Standards Board (at the address given in the 'Further Information' section at the end of this book). It currently costs £300 to apply.

Step Two: Join an Inn

This is as described above in chapter seven.

Step Three: Some or All of the Bar Standards Board Aptitude Test (if the Bar Standards Board requires it of you)

Once you have a certificate of approval from the Qualifications Committee of the Bar Standards Board, you need to apply to sit whichever parts of the aptitude test the Bar Standards Board requires of you. The **aptitude test** is run by the BPP Law School. Further information is available in the joint Bar Standards Board/ BPP Aptitude Test Booklet, available from the Bar Standards Board or BPP Law School and on their websites,[43] and past papers and

---

[43] For the booklet go to http://www.bpp.com/law/barapt_pages/bar_aptitude.htm (this page also explains very clearly what the aptitude test entails) or the Bar Standards Board's website www.barstandardsboard.org.uk.

application forms are available from the Director of the Bar Standards Board's Aptitude Test at the BPP Law School.

The test is conducted twice a year (in April and in September) with the deadline for entry to the test being the start of those months. Most of the test is prepared for by private study using the reading lists in the Aptitude Test Booklet and past papers referred to above. For those who have to do section 4 of the test (the advocacy section: see below), there is a compulsory short advocacy training course run by BPP Law School in London (this is taught in three weekend days). If the Bar Standards Board requires you to do the whole test (and training course) it will cost you about £2,150.

As it currently stands, the full aptitude test consists of the following sections (some or all of which a transferring lawyer may be required to do, as set out below):

- Section 1: a three-hour written paper on the law of contract and trusts, and another three-hour written paper on the law of tort and crime. This is not like a university law exam testing law alone. The candidate will be told the areas of law (the particular bit of contract, trusts, tort, and crime) beforehand, and at each of the two exams will be given a set of instructions, just as a barrister would get, and will have to draft a pleading (a formal document setting out a claim or defence) or opinion in these areas of law, just as a barrister would do. The candidate will then be assessed on his or her correct understanding of the law (you must get over 40 per cent on this) and drafting and communication skills (you must get 50 per cent on this). In these exams, and those in section 2, copies of any relevant statutes will be provided. The current cost of sitting these exams is £200 each.
- Section 2: A three-hour written paper on the English legal system, and another three-hour written paper on public (constitutional and administrative) and European law. These are more like university exams, testing understanding of the law itself (rather than the performance of a barrister-type written task) and giving a choice of questions. (The pass mark for these exams is 40 per cent.) The current cost of sitting these exams is £150 each.
- Section 3: A three-hour multiple-choice paper on procedure and evidence (just like one of the exams in the BVC). (You must get over 60 per cent on this exam.) The current cost of sitting this exam is £250.
- Section 4: the advocacy test: (i) An assessment of a candidate's written skeleton argument and an oral presentation of up to 12 minutes

of a mock court application (the candidate can chose whether it is on a civil or criminal law matter); (ii) an assessment of a candidate's oral examination of a witness of up to 12 minutes. (You must get over 50 per cent in each of these assessments.) The current cost of sitting this exam is £300, and the cost of the compulsory training course is £650.

• Section 5: oral questioning for up to 30 minutes on the candidate's knowledge of the Bar Code of Conduct rules. (You must get over 50 per cent in this section.) The current cost of sitting this exam is £250.

Step Four: Pupillage (if the Bar Standards Board requires it of you)

This is as described above in chapters ten and following, although those transferring do not need to go through **OLPAS**.

Further Information

GENERAL INFORMATION ABOUT A CAREER AT THE BAR

* www.barcouncil.org.uk and www.barstandardsboard.org.uk: The official (ie **Bar Council/Bar Standards Board**) sites explaining the requirements of the qualifying law degree, BVC, pupillage, and various related matters. The sites were being revamped at the time of writing, but it looks like the Bar Council's site will contain general information on becoming a barrister (including useful case studies by those who've recently come to the Bar), while the Bar Standards Board's site will contain more technical forms, regulations, pupillage checklists and lists of accredited BVC providers. The old Bar Council website had a very useful discussion forum where many of you answered each other's questions, and it looks like this will be restarted on the new websites, probably on the Bar Council site.

* Doctorjob: www.doctorjob.com/Barrister: As well as general advice of the type provided in this book, the doctorjob website provides excellent profiles of the different areas of practice as a barrister in the 'Essential information' part of the page.

* The student part of the Chambers & Partners website: www.chambersandpartners/chambersstudent: An excellent version of the timetable for becoming a barrister, good summaries of practice areas, and other useful information.

* The Bar Council produces very good brochures, *It's Your Call: A Career at the Bar* and *Bar Vocational Course*, available by writing to the Careers and Information Assistant, Bar Council, 289 High Holborn, London WC1R 5NT or by emailing careers@barcouncil.org.uk. The *It's Your Call* brochure can also be downloaded (although it's a big file at over 10Mb) from www.legaleducation.org.uk under the 'Careers' menu as item 'Online brochure'.

* The TARGET Law and *Pupillage Handbook*, published by GTI who run the BVC and pupillage online application systems, is very good.

  www.combar.co.uk: The Commercial Bar Association has good general advice about the Bar, and in particular about the commercial Bar.

  www.lawcareers.net/Barristers: General advice on coming to the Bar: Particularly good on the different Bar practice areas and alternative careers for lawyers.

  The Law Careers Advice Network: www.lcan.org.uk: Not brilliant.

  http://www.thelawyer.com/students/guide/the_bar.html: *The Lawyer* magazine's guide to the Bar: Good for statistics and a pretty good overview.

  Henry Cecil, *Brief to Counsel*, 3rd edition (London, Michael Joseph, 1958). A light-hearted explanation of the Bar and the process of becoming a barrister. If Cecil's book weren't 20 years old I might not have had to write mine.

WRITTEN FICTION CONCERNING PUPILLAGE

* Charlotte Buckhaven, *Barrister By and Large* (London, Pan Books, 1985). A witty portrayal of the trials and tribulations (pun intended) of a pupil-barrister. This is pretty accurate and Buckhaven has a sharp turn of phrase—the best description of a pupillage that I've found.

* Henry Cecil, *Brothers in Law* (London, Michael Joseph, 1955). An excellent description of a pupillage and very useful for getting to know the terminology and ways of the Bar (as well as being an entertaining story).

  Harry Mount, *My Brief Career: The Trials of a Young Lawyer* (London, Short Books, 2004). An amusing, but fictionalised, account of a rather unpleasant pupillage, although not as useful as Buckhaven's novel. Worth it for the anecdote about the pupil having to stand for an afternoon in the middle of the pupil supervisor's room so as to block the sunlight. (Don't worry, this is extremely unlikely to happen nowadays.)

KEY ORGANISATIONS

* The four Inns: www.graysinn.org.uk, www.innertemple.org.uk, www.lincolnsinn.org.uk, www.middletemple.org.uk.

* The Bar Council and Bar Standards Board: www.barcouncil.org.uk, www.barstandardsboard.org.uk.

APPLICATIONS

* CPE: www.lawcabs.ac.uk.

* BVC: www.bvconline.co.uk.

* Pupillage: www.pupillages.com (this website also contains the online version of the *Pupillages Handbook* at http://www.pupillages.com/handbook/handbook.asp). The paper version of the *Pupillages Handbook* is distributed free to all BVC students and at the National Pupillage Fair, or may be obtained by dropping into or writing to the Bar Council (289 High Holborn, London WC1R 5NT). As well as detailed information on the various chambers and their pupillages, the handbook also contains profiles of their chambers, pupillage, and practice written by various junior barristers.

LAW LIBRARIES IN LONDON

The four Inn library catalogues: http://www.graysinnlibrary.org.uk/ (Gray's and Lincoln's), http://www.innertemplelibrary.org/external. html (Inner Temple), http://www.middletemplelibrary.org.uk/ (Middle Temple).

The Institute of Advanced Legal Studies library in London on Russell Square: http://ials.sas.ac.uk/library/library.htm.

The British Library in London on Euston Road between St. Pancras and King's Cross: http://www.bl.uk/.

INFORMATION ABOUT CHAMBERS

* Chambers and Partners UK Guide: www.chambersandpartners. com/uk. One of the major directories, giving information and rankings for different chambers and barristers in different practice areas (the print version of this guide costs £75). The student section, at www.chambersandpartners/chambersstudent, gives excellent chambers reports from a student applicant's point of view, discussing the culture of chambers and the interview process, as much as the work done there.

Legal 500: www.legal500.com. Another directory ranking chambers and barristers. This one has an interesting table of barristers' charge-out rates divided by seniority of barrister and area of practice.

The Bar Directory: www.thebardirectory.co.uk (although this website contains only an abridged version of the main, telephone book-like, tome).

THE EMPLOYED BAR

*The CPS: http://www.cps.gov.uk/working/legaltraineeinfo.html.

*The Government Legal Service: www.gls.gov.uk.

The Treasury Solicitor's Department: http://www.tsol.gov.uk.

The Army Legal Service: www.armylegal.co.uk.

The RAF legal service: http://www.raf.mod.uk/legalservices.

The Bar Association for Commerce, Finance and Industry: see http://www.bacfi.org.

The Bar Association for Local Government and the Public Service: http://www.balgps.org.uk.

LEGAL NEWS

www.legalweekstudent.net, www.thelawyer.com/student and http:// www.timesonline.co.uk/section/0,,27490,00.html: news about the world of law from a student's perspective. Also read *Counsel*, the Bar Council's magazine, and *The Lawyer* and *Legal Week* newspapers.

http://www.barristermagazine.com: a magazine that usually has a few articles on current issues in the world of the Bar.

FINANCIAL AND TAX ADVICE

* The Bar Council's *Taxation and Retirement Benefits Handbook*, 4th edn (London, General Council of the Bar, 2002). The entire book can be downloaded at http://www.barcouncil.org.uk/ documents/TaxationHandbook_Aug04.pdf.

The Inland Revenue: http://www.hmrc.gov.uk.

SOLICITORS AND LEGAL EXECUTIVES

The Law Society of England and Wales: http://www.lawsociety.org. uk/home. law.

The Solicitors' Association of Higher Court Advocates: http://www. sahca.org.

The Institute of Legal Executives: http://www.ilex.org.uk/.

HISTORY AND COMMENTARY

JH Baker, *The Common Law Tradition: Lawyers, Books and the Law* (London, Hambledon Continuum, 1999). Includes an interesting discussion of the origins of the Inns, the degree of barrister-at-law, and QCs.

Raymond Cocks, *Foundations of the Modern Bar* (London, Sweet & Maxwell, 1983). A discussion of the Bar in the nineteenth century.

Walter Ellis, *The Oxbridge Conspiracy* (London, Michael Joseph, 1994). Chapter 12 surveys the extent to which, at the time of its writing, **Oxbridge** graduates dominated the Bar and judiciary.

Andrew Goodman and Clive Berridge, *The Walking Guide to Lawyers' London* (London, Blackstone, 2000). A historical guide to legal London for the explorer on foot, including lots of pictures.

John Griffin, *Seeing Justice Done: A Guide to the Law Courts and Tribunals of Central London* (London, Wildy, Simmonds & Hill, 2006). An unusual book that consists of short interviews with representatives from all the groups of people involved (however indirectly) in administering law in London (judge, barrister, solicitor, court reporter, policeman, taxi driver, etc).

RG Hamilton, *All Jangle and Riot: Barrister's History of the Bar* (Oxford, Professional Books, 1986). An interesting survey of the Bar from Roman times forward, rendered readable by focusing mainly on famous names (Cicero, Coke, Thomas Erskine, FE Smith) and anecdotes rather than on a systematic historical description, although this is also its failing. The Tibetan Temple advocacy anecdote at pp 141–3 is worth a read.

Harold Morris, *The Barrister* (London, Geoffrey Bles, 1930). An excellent light-hearted description of the Bar and pupillage, particularly useful for explaining the traditions and terminology and giving a feel for what different barristers do. Surprisingly relevant, given its age.

Thomas Woodcock, *Legal Habits: A Brief Sartorial History of Wig, Robe and Gown* (London, Ede & Ravenscroft, 2003). The entire book can be downloaded for free at http://www.edeandravenscroft. co.uk/Legal/images/site/ Legal_Habits_book.pdf.

WRITTEN FICTION CONCERNING THE BAR

Lewis Carroll, *The Hunting of the Snark: An Agony in Eight Fits, Fit the Sixth: The Barrister's Dream* (London, Macmillan, 1876). This part of the famous nonsense poem concerns a barrister's dream of a snark's defence of a pig's criminal trial by indictment (eg 'The indictment had never been clearly expressed/ And it seemed that the Snark had begun/ And had spoken three hours, before any one guessed/ What the pig was supposed to have done').

Charles Dickens, various. Probably the best recorder of the English Bar is Charles Dickens. He spent a couple of his teenage years in the 1820s unhappily working as a solicitors' clerk in Gray's Inn and, as a result, the law and lawyers pervade his writings. Of his journalistic writing, chapter 14 of *The Uncommercial Traveller* (London, Chapman & Hall, 1861) is the most apt, but almost all of his novels contain memorable legal characters. The most legal novel is the heavy-going *Bleak House*, about the long-running (fictional) dispute of *Jarndyce v Jarndyce*. Also particularly memorable are the barrister duo Carton and Stryver in the brilliant *Tale of Two Cities* (London, Chapman & Hall, 1859), in which Carton does his best thinking drunk and with a wet towel around his head (see Book 2, Chapter 5), and the barrister Jaggers in *Great Expectations* (London, Chapman & Hall, 1861). A good map of Dickensian London, with a reference to all the (legal and non-legal) places and in which novels they appear, can be found at http://www.fidnet.com/~dap1955/dickens/dickens_london_map.html. For more information on Dickens and the Bar, see William S Holdsworth, *Charles Dickens as a Legal Historian* (New Haven, Yale University Press, 1928).

Henry Cecil, *various* (1948–1977). Real-life judge Henry Cecil Leon wrote over 20 legal novels set in and around the English Bar, influencing Mortimer and others who came after him. Lightly written, they convey well the type of thinking involved in a barrister's legal work as well as the world in which barristers move. The best loved may be the Roger Thursby novels, following him from pupillage (*Brothers in Law*) to silk (*Friends at Court*) to the bench (*Sober as a Judge*): I would highly recommend the first two as some of the best portrayals of what a civil barrister does (even including an appeal to the Court of Appeal on a point of law, which is something that is rarely covered in books and television). Most of the series are published in paperback by House of Stratus publishing.

John Mortimer's Rumpole of the Bailey stories (1978–present). Various collections of stories about the loveable criminal barrister with a penchant for Wordsworth and claret were published over a 30-year period by Mortimer, himself an experienced QC as well as a writer. The public's (not inaccurate) perception of the criminal Bar is derived almost entirely from these stories and the television series that accompanied them (see below).

Bess Willingham, *The Bedevilled Barrister* (New York, Zebra, 1999). A romance novel featuring a square-jawed barrister. Some of the heaving bosoms overlook Lincoln's Inn, but otherwise there's not much of legal interest here.

BIOGRAPHY

Lord Denning, *The Family Story* (London, Butterworths, 1981). There are many interesting and well-written legal biographies and autobiographies out there, but it is hard to beat this pithy autobiography by probably the most significant and distinctive judge of the last hundred years. The (fairly short) sections on Denning's meteoric rise through the Bar and to the benches of the highest courts in the land are of particular interest.

LAW LONDON

Mark Herber, *Legal London: A Pictorial History* (Chichester, Phillimore & Co, 1999): As the title suggests.

FILM, TELEVISION, AND RADIO

Year	Film/programme	Format	Description formats	Available
1955	Brothers in Law play	Radio		None
1956–1964	Boyd QC	TV series	78 episodes in ITV's first stab at creating the TV barrister.	None

Year	Film/programme	Format	Description formats	Available
1957	Brothers in Law	Film	Starring Ian Carmichael and Richard Attenborough. A light-hearted adaptation giving a surprisingly familiar portrayal of pupillage.	Video, DVD
1962	Brothers in Law	TV series	13-episode BBC series with Richard Briers in his first starring role.	None
1962	Trial and Error (aka The Dock Brief)	Film	A fairly dark yet whimsical film starring Richard Attenborough and Peter Sellers and adapted from a John Mortimer play.	Video, DVD
1970–1972	Brothers in Law series	Radio	39-episodes on BBC Radio 4, starring Richard Briers again.	None
1975	Rumpole and the Confession	TV show	A one-off show screened by the BBC starring Leo McKern	Video, DVD (as 'Rumpole of the Bailey —the Lost Episode' and 'Rumpole of the Bailey —the Specials')
1978–1992	Rumpole of	TV series	44 episodes adapted by Thames the Bailey from John Mortimer's stories, with Leo McKern well cast as Horace Rumpole in all of them.	Video, DVD
1980	Rumpole: the Splendours and Miseries of an Old Bailey Hack	Radio series	13 episodes, adapted from the TV series, starring Maurice Denham.	None
1992	A Few Good Men	Film	An American film about American navy lawyers (starring Tom Cruise and Jack Nicholson). Nothing to do with barristers or the English and Welsh Bar but it is my favourite law film. Sorry!	Video, DVD

Year	Film/programme	Format	Description formats	Available
1994	Law and Disorder	TV series	Six ITV episodes starring Penelope Keith.	None
1995– 2001	Kavanagh QC	TV series	A first-rate television series starring the superb, recently deceased, John Thaw.	Video, DVD
1996– 1997, 2007	This Life	TV series	33 episodes (plus a reunion episode in 2007) of a gritty but otherwise *Friends*-type cult series about a house-share of trainee solicitors and pupil barristers (Miles and Anna).	Video, DVD
2001– 2007	Judge John Deed	TV series	An interesting portrayal of the colourful life of the Bar and courts from the High Court judge's point of view, starring Martin Shaw.	DVD
2003	Rumpole and the Primrose Path	Radio series	Four radio plays of the Rumpole stories starring Timothy West and Prunella Scales.	CD
2004– 2005	The Brief	TV series	So far two ITV series of four episodes starring Alan Davies as the floppy-haired criminal barrister addicted to gambling. Notable for a fairly realistic representation of the leader–junior relationship and the small-worldliness of the Bar (everyone is related by blood or previous marriages to everyone else), and for affording many glimpses of familiar walking and drinking establishments in the Temple.	None yet
2006– 2007	New Street Law	TV series	A BBC series of eight episodes set in the world of the criminal Bar in Manchester, starring John Hannah.	None yet

Glossary

advice • as a noun this refers to a written piece of advice drafted by a barrister, also called an **opinion**.

advocacy • arguing cases (in court or other arenas).

advocate • in England and Wales, anyone who argues cases; in Scotland, the technical term for what is called a barrister in England and Wales.

appear, appearance • going to court on behalf of a client is called 'appearing' in court.

aptitude test • the **Bar Standards Board's** set of examinations for foreign lawyers and English or Welsh solicitors who want to transfer to the Bar. The training course for the **advocacy** part of this test is provided by the BPP Law School in London.

arbitration • a popular alternative to the legal system as a way of solving disputes, still employing an impartial judge or judges (the arbitrator(s)) but taking place in private and with less formal rules of procedure and evidence.

assessed mini-pupillage • a **mini-pupillage** in which the pupil is formally assessed by the chambers, and which therefore forms part of the application process if the mini-pupil ever applies for pupillage.

attorney • this term is not used in the UK. It is an archaic reference to solicitors who practised in the courts of **Chancery**, when such courts were separate to the courts of Law. It is also the US term for lawyer.

audience • a right of audience is a right to be heard in a court. Although everyone has the right to speak in court on their own behalf, only those with rights of audience have the right to speak in court on behalf of others. See also **higher rights of audience**.

BA • Bachelor of Arts undergraduate degree. Most undergraduate law students are awarded an *LLB*, but some universities call their degree a BA. Neither is better than the other.

bands • a neckband with two cloth strips hanging from it, worn by barristers when in the higher courts.

the Bar • the collective term for all barristers. This can also be qualified, eg 'the London Bar', 'the criminal Bar'.

Bar Co • the Bar Services Company, set up by the **Bar Council** to get barristers good deals on banking and other products.

Bar Council • the General Council of the Bar of England and Wales, the professional organisation of all barristers.

barrister-at-law • the degree granted by an **Inn** that renders a person a barrister.

Bar Pro Bono Unit • a charity that organises the provision of **pro bono** work by putting those in need in touch with barristers willing to do such work.

Bar school • the informal term for the institution at which the **Bar Vocational Course** is studied.

Bar Standards Board or BSB • a statutory body, made up of 15 members of whom a majority are not barristers, which was recently set up to act as independent regulator of the Bar, with the **Bar Council** retaining its function as the representative of barristers for the purposes of consultation and lobbying etc. Qualification as a barrister and the **Code of Conduct** fall within the remit of the BSB, although some of the day-to-day administration is still performed through the Bar Council.

Bar Vocational Course or BVC • the compulsory year-long course of practical legal training, after academic study and before **pupillage**.

before • in front of, with regard to a judge, eg 'I **appeared** before Judge Smith this morning'.

the bench • the **judiciary** (so called because they sit behind a bench).

Bencher or master of the bench • a senior member of an **Inn**, usually a **silk** or judge.

brief • as a noun this denotes either the document containing the instructions to the solicitor or, more broadly, a case; as a verb, to **instruct** a barrister.

brief fee • the pay that the barrister gets for a particular instruction.

BSB • see **Bar Standards Board**.

BVC • see **Bar Vocational Course**.

cab rank rule • the rule providing that barristers cannot turn away work when it is suitable and they have time to do it.

call • short for **call to the Bar**. Alternatively, used to refer to how long ago a barrister's *call to the Bar* was, as a measure of his or her seniority (as in 'He's four years call').

call to the Bar or *call night* • the ceremony by which your **Inn** grants you the degree of **barrister-at-law**, although you are not entitled to practise as a barrister until you have completed your **pupillage**. See also **deferred call**.

Career Development Loan • a loan scheme sponsored by the government in which the interest is repaid by the government for as long as the course continues.

chambers (treated as singular) • a collection of barristers grouped together for convenience and marketing. The closest barristerial equivalent to a solicitors' **firm** or a company. Set is a synonym, although 'chambers' is the more common word.

chambers tea • a traditional gathering of the members of a **chambers** for tea at a particular time. Only some chambers maintain this tradition.

Chancery • historically one of two separate systems of courts administering a separate system of law (called 'Equity' rather than 'the Common Law'). Nowadays the term refers to a type of legal work that concentrates upon wills, property, trusts, and companies, and the **sets** that do such work (which, in London, are mainly based in Lincoln's Inn).

circuits • the regional associations of barristers and courts.

clerk • barristers' employees who provide various support services including arranging the barristers' diaries and negotiating the barristers' fees.

Code of Conduct • a code set down and amended by the **Bar Standards Board** which governs ethical and related rules of practice for barristers.

collarette • the female barrister's collar, to be worn in the higher courts.

Common Professional Examination • see **CPE**.

con • a common abbreviation for 'conference' (for **juniors**) or 'consultation' (for **silks**), which can refer to any professional meeting with clients or other barristers (including a **telecon**).

Continuing Professional Development • see **CPD**.

counsel (singular and plural) • one or more barristers.

court shirt • also known as a **tunic shirt**, the collarless shirt worn (together with the separate collar attached by studs) by barristers in the higher courts.

CPD • the scheme by which barristers must do a certain number of activities every year as part of their **Continuing Professional Development**.

CPE or *Common Professional Examination* • one of the names of the one-year conversion course undertaken after a non-law degree and before a **Bar Vocational Course**. See also **GDL**.

CPS or *Crown Prosecution Service* • the Government department which is behind just about every criminal prosecution and instructs both employed barristers within its ranks and self-employed barristers in private practice.

deferred call • a proposed new system for **call to the Bar**, at the time of writing due for implementation for those starting the **BVC** in 2008, although it is always possible that the deferred call proposals will be scrapped. Under the new system, people would be called the Bar when they complete their **pupillage** (with a **temporary call** halfway through), in contrast to the current system under which they are called to the Bar a year earlier upon completion of the BVC.

devil or *devilling* • a devil is one paid by another barrister to do his work without being herself **instructed** by the client. Note also that pupils in Scotland are called 'devils' (with pupil-supervisors being 'devilmasters').

dining and *dinners* • eating dinners in one's **Inn** so as to accrue the necessary qualifying sessions to be called to the Bar.

Diploma in Law • another name for the **GDL**.

disbar • to remove a barrister's right to practise as a barrister.

dock brief • traditionally, a criminal defendant without a solicitor has the right to choose any barrister in court to represent him for a fixed rate paid for by the government. This is a 'dock brief' because the barrister is instructed from the dock (where the accused stands).

domus • the part of the evening accompanying a **dinner** in the **Inn** (consisting of a **moot**, debate, speech, or performance) and which, together with the dinner, makes up a **qualifying session**.

door tenant • a barrister (often an academic) who is an associate of **chambers** but not a member of chambers and does not take rooms in chambers (because he or she practises abroad, is effectively retired, or has another career).

Employed Bar • the collection of all barristers who are employed (ie employees), rather than self-employed. Compare with the **self-employed Bar**.

exempting law degree • a four-year undergraduate law degree that also incorporates the **BVC**. Currently offered only by Northumbria University.

fee note • a barrister's invoice.

firm • a partnership of solicitors.

first six • a six-month **pupillage** granted by a **chambers**, where that period amounts to the first six months of the one-year pupillage requirement. This is the non-practising period of pupillage, in which the pupil is not entitled to practise as a barrister.

Free Representation Unit or *FRU* • a non-governmental organisation that provides free representation in employment and other **tribunals** to those in need, largely by Bar students, pupils, and junior barristers.

GDL or *Graduate Diploma in Law* • One of the names of the one-year conversion course undertaken after a non-law degree and before a **BVC**. See also **CPE**.

Government Legal Service or *GLS* • the umbrella organisation in which most of the government's lawyers (eg those working for HM Revenue & Customs or for the Treasury) are found, although the Foreign Office employs its lawyers separately, as does the **CPS**.

Gray's Inn • one of the four **Inns of Court.**

head of chambers • the barrister who acts as the figurehead of the **chambers**.

hearing • a formal session in a court or **tribunal** in which a judge makes a decision about something.

higher rights of audience • the right to **appear** in the Crown Courts, High Court, Court of Appeal, and House of Lords. All barristers have such rights, but solicitors must do specialist exams to get them (and if they do they become **solicitor-advocates**).

independent Bar • the old name for the collection of all self-employed (rather than employed) barristers, now **the self-employed Bar**.

Inner Temple • one of the four **Inns of Court.**

Inns of Court or *Inns* • every barrister is a member of one of the four Inns and was granted the title of barrister by that Inn after **dining** in the Inn a certain number of times. The Inns provide social and library facilities to barristers, and scholarships to would-be barristers. Not to be confused with the Inns of Court School of Law, which historically was linked to the Inns of Court but now is just one of the many **Bar schools**.

instruct • to engage a barrister, the terms of the engagement being the 'instructions'.

instructing solicitors • the solicitors who have engaged a particular barrister on a particular case.

intellectual property • rights of authors and creators that are protected through the law of copyright, patents, and trademarks.

judge shadowing or *judge marshalling* • a short period of work experience spent with a judge.

judiciary • the body of judges.

junior clerk • a junior **clerk**, often dealing with the more menial tasks like carrying files to court or assisting with photocopying.

junior • a barrister who is not yet a **silk**.

KC or King's Counsel • a **silk** when the reigning monarch is a king and not a queen.

keep terms • undertake the requisite number of **qualifying sessions** (mainly **dinners**) to qualify as a barrister.

Law Society • the solicitors' regulatory body (and their equivalent of the **Bar Council**).

lay client • the person or company with the legal problem or dispute, as opposed to the solicitors who are known as the **professional client**.

leader and *being led* • a leader is a senior barrister also instructed by the same party on the same case, under whom you work (and by whom you are 'being led'). Your leader will often be a **silk**, but will sometimes be a senior **junior**, that is a non-silk who is more senior than you. On big cases there may be more than two barristers, and so a chain from most the senior, through the barrister or barristers who are both being led and themselves leading, down to the most junior who is only being led.

legal executive • similar to a solicitor but with a different qualification route.

Legal Practice Course • see **LPC**.

licensed access • a scheme by which, as an exception to the general rule, an organisation (such as a local council) may **instruct** barristers directly.

Lincoln's Inn • one of the four **Inns of Court**.

litigant-in-person • a slightly clumsy phrase used to describe a person who appears in court on his or her own behalf, without a solicitor or barrister. As one would expect, this is more common in smaller cases.

litigation • legal disputes, in contrast with what is called 'advisory' work or 'non-contentious' work.

LLB • Bachelor of Laws undergraduate law degree. See also **BA**.

LLM • Master of Laws master's level law degree.

LPC or Legal Practice Course • The course for training to become a solicitor; the equivalent of the **BVC**.

magistrate • a person without legal training who sits as a judge part time in the lower criminal courts.

master of the bench • see **Bencher.**

mess • the square of four people in which one is seated at an **Inn dinner.**

Middle Temple • one of the four **Inns of Court.**

mini-pupil • someone doing a **mini-pupillage.**

mini-pupillage or *mini* • work experience at a barrister's **chambers.**

moot, mooting • mock legal arguments, often mock appeals rather than full trials.

noting brief • when a barrister or pupil is instructed to attend court in order to take notes of what transpires.

Old Bailey • the sixteenth-century court near St Paul's Cathedral now officially known as the Central Criminal Court in London. Named after the original name of the street where it stands (which was named after the city wall, or 'bailey').

OLPAS • the online pupillage application scheme.

opinion • the same as an *advice.*

Oxbridge • a collective term for the ancient universities of Oxford and Cambridge.

pension • the collective formal meetings of an **Inn**'s **Benchers.**

PgDL • Post-graduate Diploma in Law. Another name for the **GDL.**

practice • a barrister's or solicitor's 'practice' is the totality of the work that he or she does.

practice manager • a modern term for **clerk.**

pro bono • short for 'pro bono publico', which means 'for the public good', this term refers to doing cases for free for those who cannot afford to pay as a kind of charity work.

professional client • the solicitor who has instructed you, as opposed to the *lay client.*

professional indemnity insurance • the insurance policy that barristers must take out to protect them if they get sued for causing harm by negligent work.

public law • constitutional and administrative law, often with human rights and planning law.

pupil or *pupil barrister* • a barrister doing his **pupillage** under the supervision of a **pupil supervisor**.

pupillage • the one-year period of apprenticeship to becoming a barrister.

pupillage award • the money paid by a **chambers** to its **pupils** during **pupillage**.

pupillage checklist • the **Bar Standards Board**'s checklist setting out what the pupil has done and seen during pupillage. This must be completed by **pupils** before they may be granted a certificate to practise.

pupil supervisor • the person to whom a **pupil** is apprenticed during his or her **pupillage**. Pupil supervisors used to be called 'pupilmasters' until recently.

QC or *Queen's Counsel* • a higher-ranked barrister, also known as a **silk**. See also **KC**.

qualifying law degree • a law degree that satisfies the **Bar Standards Board**'s requirements and so can form part of the training to become a barrister.

qualifying session • an **Inn**-organised event that counts towards the requisite number of units that must be completed before **call to the Bar**.

RCJ • see **Royal Courts of Justice**.

rights of audience • see **audience** and **higher rights of audience**.

Royal Courts of Justice or *RCJ* • the central civil court building on Fleet Street, containing much of the High Court and the Civil Division of the Court of Appeal.

second six • a six-month **pupillage** granted by a **chambers**, where that period amounts to the second six months of the one-year pupillage requirement, following on (perhaps with a gap in between) from a **first six**. This is the practising period of pupillage, in which a **pupil** is entitled to practise as a barrister with the permission and supervision of his or her **pupil supervisor**.

self-employed Bar • the collection of all barristers who are self-employed (which makes up the majority). Compare with the **Employed Bar**. Formerly referred to as the **independent Bar**.

senior counsel • a **QC** or **KC**.

senior status law degree • a two-year law degree taken after doing a non-law degree. Basically a more in-depth version of the **CPE** or **GDL**.

serjeant-at-law • a senior rank of barrister which existed until the late nineteenth century and from which rank all judges were chosen.

set • See **chambers**.

silk • a **QC** or **KC** (so called because the silk gown they wear).

skeleton argument or *'skelly'* • a written argument set out in points (rather than as a speech) that is submitted to the court before an oral hearing so that the judge and the opponent know what is being argued and so that the oral argument need not take as long as it otherwise would.

solicitor • a member of the other branch of the legal profession.

solicitor-advocates • solicitors with **higher rights of audience** (which they obtain by passing special examinations).

Specialist Bar Associations • associations of barristers practising in a particular field which provide lectures and **advocacy** training to their members.

sponsor • a barrister assigned to you by your **Inn** to help advise you as you are going through the various stages of becoming a barrister.

St Dunstan's House • the building currently housing the Commercial and Technology and Construction divisions of the High Court, on New Fetter Lane near Fleet Street in London (although due to be replaced in the next couple of years).

taken on • what happens when a **pupil** is granted **tenancy** by his or her **chambers**.

take silk • to become a **QC** or **KC**.

telecon • a telephone conference (ie conversation). See also **con**.

the Temple • the area south of Fleet Street and near Temple tube station which contains two of the **Inns of Court**, namely **Middle Temple** and **Inner Temple**.

temporary call • a provisional **call to the Bar** after six months of pupillage, to enable practise as a barrister during the **second six** months of **pupillage** under the proposed new **deferred call** system.

tenancy (and *tenant*) • the membership of a **chambers** of a barrister (note that a **pupil barrister**, who is a **pupil** but not a **tenant**).

third six • a third period of six months of **pupillage**. Not necessary in order to qualify, and so usually undertaken only if a **pupil** is not offered **tenancy** after a **second six** or does not want tenancy at the chambers in which he or she did the second six.

training contract • the two-year period of training that one undertakes to become a solicitor; the equivalent to the barrister's (one-year) **pupillage**.

Treasurer • the senior member of an **Inn**.

tribunal • a body that is like a court but less formal, set up by statutes to deal with particular types of hearing more cheaply than a court could. Also a more generic term used to refer to all courts and similar decision-making bodies.

tunic shirt • see **court shirt**.

usher • a court official who administers the courts, doing clerical duties, calling cases into court, administering the oath to witnesses, etc.

utter barrister • the technical rank of a barrister (rather than a **pupil**), although this term has fallen out of use. This is what it will say on your certificate of **call**.

watching brief • a **brief** to watch court or other proceedings (and take notes on them) but not to take part in those proceedings.

Timetables for Routes to the Bar

Steps to take	Time of Year (you may want to write in the relevant years that apply to you)	Route A: Law graduates: Law degree, then BVC, then Pupillage	Route B: Non-law graduates: Non-law degree, then CPE or GDL, then BVC, then Pupillage	Route C: Other things: Law degree, then other things, then BVC, then Pupillage
Deadline for CPE/GDL applications	January . . .	n/a		n/a
National Pupillage Fair (with mini-pupillages in mind)	March . . .	. . . during the penultimate year of your degree course	. . . of the final year of degree course.	. . . during the penultimate year before your BVC.
Start to apply for mini-pupillages	April . . .			
Deadline for Inns' CPE/GDL scholarships	April . . .	n/a		n/a
Prime time for mini-pupillages	summer to March . . .	. . . during the final year of your degree course	. . . during your CPE/GDL.	. . . during the year before your BVC.
Law fairs (for info on BVC programmes)	autumn . . .			
Deadline for Inns' Junior Scholarships applications	November . . .			
Deadline for BVC Applications	January . . .			
BVC offers made	March . . .			
National Pupillage Fair (with pupillages in mind	March . . .			
Deadline for OLPAS summer season	March . . .			
Inns' Junior Scholarship interviews	April . . .			
Deadline for joining an Inn	May . . .			
OLPAS summer offers	August . . .	. . . just after the end of your degree course	. . . just after the end of your CPE/GDL.	

BVC begins	September...			
Deadline for OLPAS autumn season	September...			
OLPAS autumn offers	November...			
Deadline for Inns' Senior Scholarships applications	July...	...during your. BVC	...during your BVC.	...during your BVC.
Inns' Senior Scholarships interviews	September...			
First Six months of pupillage	October...	...during your pupillage.	...during your pupillage.	...during your pupillage.
Second Six months of pupillage	April...			
Steps to take	*Time of Year* (you may want to write in the relevant years that apply to you)	*Route A: Law graduates:* Law degree, then BVC, then Pupillage	*Route B: Non-law graduates:* Non-law degree, then CPE or GDL, then BVC, then Pupillage	*Route C: Other things:* Law degree, then other things, then BVC, then Pupillage

NB: References in the table to a particular year (such as your final undergraduate year, BVC year, pupillage year, etc) are references to the academic September-to-August year, not the calendar year. Also, do not think that this timetable is set in stone: for example, many people do mini-pupillages before the year before their BVC, and continue doing mini-pupillages and applying for pupillages during and after their BVC.

INDEX